M000032993

The
Poodle

An Owner's Guide To

A HAPPY HEALTHY PET

Howell Book House

Howell Book House
A Simon & Schuster Macmillan Company
1633 Broadway
New York, NY 10019

Library of Congress Cataloging-in-Publication Data
Guidry, Virginia Parker.
The poodle : an owner's guide to a happy, healthy pet / Virginia Parker Guidry.

p. cm.
Includes bibliographical references.

ISBN 0-87605-387-8

1. Poodles. I. Title.
SF429.P85G85 1995
636.7'2—dc20   95-434

       CIP

Manufactured in the United States of America
10 9 8 7 6 5 4 3 2 1

Series Director: Dominique De Vito
Series Assistant Director: Felice Primeau
Book Design: Michele Laseau
Cover Design: Iris Jeromnimon
Illustration: Jeff Yesh
Photography:
   Cover by Kerrin Winter & Dale Churchill; puppy by Pets by Paulette
   Joan Balzarini: 96
   Mary Bloom: 26, 96, 136, 145
   Paulette Braun/Pets by Paulette: 5, 7, 29, 34–35, 36, 39, 42, 64, 96
   Buckinghamhill American Cocker Spaniels: 148
   Courtesy of the American Kennel Club: 14, 17, 19, 20, 21, 22
   Sian Cox: 43, 51, 52, 61, 63, 90, 134
   Dr. Ian Dunbar: 98, 101, 103, 111, 116–117, 122, 123, 127
   Dan Lyons: 8, 12, 96
   Cathy Merrithew: 129
   Liz Palika: 133
   Janice Raines: 132
   Susan Rezy: 96–97
   Judith Strom: 2–3, 11. 27, 30, 48, 54, 57, 58, 71, 84, 96, 107, 110, 128, 130, 135, 137,
   139, 140, 144, 149, 150
   Kerrin Winter/Dale Churchill: 9, 23, 25, 66
Production Team: Troy Barnes, John Carroll, Jama Carter,
   Kathleen Caulfield, Trudy Coler, Victor Peterson, Terri Sheehan,
   Marvin Van Tiem, Amy DeAngelis and Kathy Iwasaki

Contents

Welcome

to the

World

of the

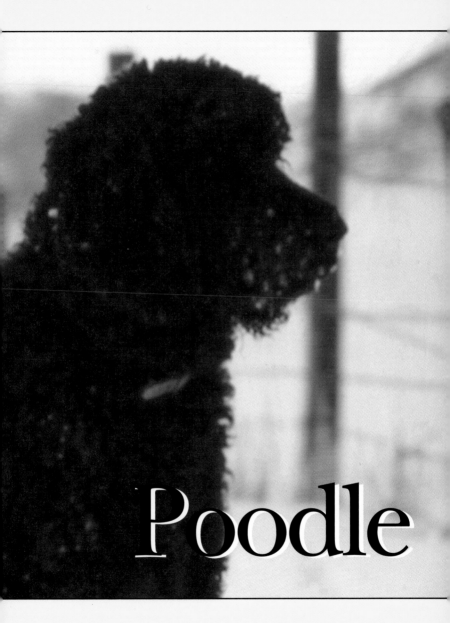

Poodle

External Features of the Poodle

Muzzle
Stop
Cheek
Shoulder
Skull
Crest
Neck
Forearm
Wrist
Withers
Back
Pastern
Dewclaw
Elbow
Loin
Knee
Croup
Toes
Hock

chapter 1

What

is a

Poodle?

No dog surpasses the Poodle in intelligence; in fact, no dog is his equal. He has a quality of mind that borders on the human; his reasoning powers are evident to all with whom he is associated, and there is apparently no limit to his aptitude for learning.

William A. Bruette
The Complete Dog Book

What exactly is a Poodle? How do we know what a Poodle should look like? How should it act? What about size and color? How does it differ from other breeds of dogs?

To find the answers to these questions, we look to what is called a "breed standard."

The breed standard is an important reference point for dog breeders because it gives an overall picture. By outlining the specifics of a particular breed of dog, breeders nationwide are able to strive

5

toward one goal, though interpretations may vary. This allows for consistency within the breed and for dogs that reflect the best of a breed.

Follow along with a look at the Official Standard for the Poodle, which was approved by the American Kennel Club on August 14, 1984, and reformatted March 27, 1990, by the Poodle Club of America. This is where we look to truly understand the Poodle, at least in the literal sense. You will find that some understanding of the Poodle is subjective, and you will have to learn this through living and sharing a home with the dog. In the following discussion, the sections in italics are taken directly from the standard; the rest is commentary.

WHAT IS A BREED STANDARD?

A breed standard—a detailed description of an individual breed—is meant to portray the *ideal* specimen of that breed. This includes ideal structure, temperament, gait, type—all aspects of the dog. Because the standard describes an ideal specimen, it isn't based on any particular dog. It is a concept against which judges compare actual dogs and breeders strive to produce dogs. At a dog show, the dog that wins is the one that comes closest, in the judge's opinion, to the standard for its breed. Breed standards are written by the breed parent clubs, the national organizations formed to oversee the well-being of the breed. They are voted on and approved by the members of the parent clubs.

General Appearance, Carriage and Condition

The Poodle today, according to the breed standard, is *a very active, intelligent and elegant-appearing dog, squarely built, well proportioned, moving soundly and carrying himself proudly. Properly clipped in the traditional fashion and carefully groomed, the Poodle has about him an air of distinction and dignity peculiar to himself.*

This paragraph describes the essence of the breed, rather than pinpointing anything in particular. It is an overview of what the Poodle should be, in mind, body and spirit.

SIZE, PROPORTION, SUBSTANCE

Size: The Standard, Miniature and Toy Poodles are not separate breeds. Rather, they are the three different sizes of one breed.

The Standard Poodle is over 15 inches at the highest point of the shoulders. Any Poodle which is 15 inches or less in height shall be disqualified from competition as a Standard Poodle.

The Miniature Poodle is 15 inches or under at the highest point of the shoulders, with a minimum height in excess of 10 inches. Any Poodle which is over 15 inches or is 10 or less at the highest point of the shoulders shall be disqualified from competition as a Miniature Poodle.

With the variety of colors and sizes, the combinations are endless!

The Toy Poodle is 10 inches or under at the highest point of the shoulders. Any Poodle which is more than 10 inches at the highest point of the shoulders shall be disqualified from competition as a Toy Poodle.

As long as the Toy Poodle is definitely a Toy Poodle, and the Miniature Poodle a Miniature Poodle, both in balance and proportion for the Variety, diminutiveness shall be the deciding factor when all other points are equal.

The variety of sizes is perhaps the most unique aspect of the Poodle. This allows potential owners to select a size that best meets their particular needs, whether living in an apartment or a home with a large yard. How many other breeds can make such a claim?

Proportion: *To insure the desirable squarely built appearance, the length of body measured from the breastbone to the point of the rump approximates the height from the highest point of the shoulders to the ground.*

Substance: *Bone and muscle of both forelegs and hindlegs are in proportion to size of dog.*

HEAD AND EXPRESSION

The Poodle's eyes *are very dark, oval in shape and set far enough apart and positioned to create an alert, intelligent expression. Major fault: eyes round, protruding, large or very light.*

The ears should be *hanging close to the head, set at or slightly below eye level. The ear leather is long, wide and thickly feathered; however, the ear fringe should not be of excessive length.*

The Poodle's skull is *moderately rounded, with a slight but definite stop. Cheekbones and muscles flat. Length from occiput to stop about the same as length of muzzle.*

The muzzle is *long, straight and fine, with slight chiseling under the eyes. Strong without lippiness. The chin definite enough to preclude snipiness. Major fault: lack of chin.*

The teeth are white, strong and with a scissors bite. Major fault: undershot, overshot, wry mouth.

A Poodle with a proper head and face looks dignified.

The Poodle's face, the look in its eyes and its overall expression, is one of its most noticed features. And for good reason: The face and head of a well-bred Poodle are a beautiful sight. If in doubt, spend an afternoon strolling through a dog show, watching and paying close attention to the Poodles. Study the faces and get a feeling for their expressions. There is a big difference between the face of a Poodle bred with the above standard in mind and one that is the product of a careless breeding.

NECK, TOPLINE, BODY

The Poodle's neck is *well proportioned, strong and long enough to permit the head to be carried high and with dignity, skin snug at throat. The neck rises from strong, smoothly muscled shoulders. Major fault: ewe neck.*

The topline is *level, neither sloping nor roached, from the highest point of the shoulder blade to the base of the tail, with the exception of a slight hollow just behind the shoulder.*

The Poodle's body includes a *chest deep and moderately wide with well sprung ribs. The loin is short, broad and muscular. The tail is straight, set on high and carried up, docked of sufficient length to insure a balanced outline. Major fault: set low, curled or carried over the back.*

FOREQUARTERS

The Poodle should have *strong, smoothly muscled shoulders. The shoulder blade is well laid back and approximately the same length as the upper foreleg. Major fault: steep shoulder.*

The forelegs are *straight and parallel when viewed from the front. When viewed from the side the elbow is directly below the highest point of the shoulder. The pasterns are strong. Dewclaws may be removed.*

This Poodle can stand proud of its elegant body.

The feet *are rather small, oval in shape with toes well arched and cushioned on thick firm pads. Nails short but not excessively shortened. The feet turn neither in nor out. Major fault: paper or splay foot.*

HINDQUARTERS

The angulation of the hindquarters balances that of the forequarters. Hind legs straight and parallel when viewed from the rear. Muscular with width in the region of the stifles, which are well bent: femur and tibia are about equal in length; hock to heel short and perpendicular to the ground. When standing, the rear toes are only slightly behind the point of the rump. Major fault: cow hocks.

COAT

The Poodle's coat is spectacular, especially when coiffed for show. The breed standard calls for a coat quality that is *(1) Curly: of naturally harsh texture, dense throughout. (2) Corded: hanging in tight even cords of varying length; longer on mane or body coat, head and ears; shorter on puffs, bracelets, and pompoms.*

A Poodle under 12 months may be shown in the "Puppy" clip. In all regular classes, Poodles 12 months or over must be shown in the "English Saddle" or "Continental" clip. In the Stud Dog and Brood Bitch classes and in a noncompetitive Parade of Champions, Poodles may be shown in the "Sporting Clip" clip. A Poodle shown in any other type of clip shall be disqualified.

THE AMERICAN KENNEL CLUB

Familiarly referred to as "the AKC," the American Kennel Club is a nonprofit organization devoted to the advancement of purebred dogs. The AKC maintains a registry of recognized breeds and adopts and enforces rules for dog events including shows, obedience trials, field trials, hunting tests, lure coursing, herding, earthdog trials, agility and the Canine Good Citizen program. It is a club of clubs, established in 1884 and composed, today, of over 500 autonomous dog clubs throughout the United States. Each club is represented by a delegate; the delegates make up the legislative body of the AKC, voting on rules and electing directors. The American Kennel Club maintains the Stud Book, the record of every dog ever registered with the AKC, and publishes a variety of materials on purebred dogs, including a monthly magazine, books and numerous educational pamphlets. For more information, contact the AKC at the address listed in Chapter 13, "Resources," and look for the names of their publications in Chapter 12, "Recommended Reading."

Puppy Clip: *Poodles under a year old may be shown in the Puppy clip with the coat long. The face, throat, feet and base of the tail are shaved. The entire shaven foot is visible. There is a pompom on the end of the tail. In order to give a neat appearance and a smooth unbroken line, shaping of the coat is permissible.*

English Saddle: *In the English Saddle clip, the face, throat, feet, forelegs and base of the tail are shaved, leaving puffs on the forelegs and a pompom on the end of the tail. The hindquarters are covered with a short blanket of hair except for a curved, shaved area on each flank and two shaved bands on each hind leg. The entire shaven foot and a portion of the shaven leg above the puff are visible. The rest of the body is left in full coat but may be shaped in order to insure overall balance.*

Continental: *In the Continental clip, the face, throat, feet and base of the tail are shaved. The hindquarters are shaved with pompoms (optional) on the hips. The legs are shaved, leaving bracelets on the hind legs and puffs on the forelegs. There is a pompom on the end of the tail. The entire shaven foot and a portion of the shaven foreleg above the puff are visible. The rest of the body is left in full coat but may be shaped to insure overall balance.*

Sporting: *The Sporting clip calls for the Poodle's face, feet, throat and base of tail shaved, leaving a scissored cap on the top of the head and a pompom on the end of the tail. The rest*

*of the body and legs are clipped or scissored to follow that out-
line of the dog, leaving a short blanket of coat no longer than
one inch in length. The hair on the legs may be slightly longer
than that on the body.*

*In all clips, the hair of the topknot may either be left free or
held in place by elastic bands. The hair is only of sufficient
length to present a smooth outline. "Topknot" refers only to
hair on the skull, from stop to occiput. This is the only area
where elastic bands may be used.*

Besides its expressive face, the Poodle is probably most
noted for its thick, curly coat and elaborate trims. The
show-ring-coat styles we know today can be traced to
antiquity—and to a purpose. Originally a water dog,
early Poodles had heavy, water-repellent coats that
helped keep them warm while dashing in and out of
water retrieving game for their hunting masters. But
the dense coats often hampered the dog's movement
once wet. The solution was to trim the hair short on
the hindquarters and leave it full around the dog's
chest for warmth. Show trims, and the myriad pet trims
seen today, evolved from this utilitarian purpose.

*Pet Poodles
generally do
not sport
elaborate clips.*

COLOR

Not only do Poodles come in
three sizes, but they can be found
in a rainbow of coat colors.
According to the breed standard,
*the coat is an even and solid color at
the skin. In blues, grays, silvers,
browns, café-au-laits, apricots and
creams the coat may show varying
shades of the same color. This is frequently present in the somewhat
darker feathering of the ears and in
the tipping of the ruff. While clear
colors are definitely preferred, such
natural variation in the shading of
the coat is not to be considered a fault.*

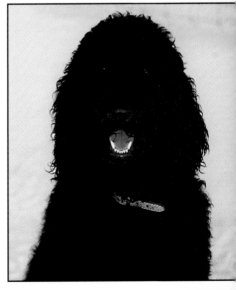

*Brown and café-au-lait Poodles have liver-colored noses, eye-
rims and lips, dark toenails and dark amber eyes. Black, blue,*

gray, silver, cream and white Poodles have black noses, eye-rims and lips, black or self-colored toenails and very dark eyes. In the apricots, while the foregoing coloring is preferred, liver-colored noses, eye-rims and lips, and amber eyes are permitted. Major fault: color of nose, lips and eye-rims incomplete, or of wrong color for color of dog.

Parti-colored dogs shall be disqualified. The coat of a parti-colored dog is not an even solid color at the skin but is of two or more colors.

This Standard displays her neatly trimmed curly coat.

Generally, black and white are the most common colors; locating a brown, apricot or silver Poodle can be more difficult. Although the Poodle standard does allow for myriad colors, breeders trying to produce one distinctively solid color may have problems. Many of the accepted colors are products of recessive genes and dilutions that bring with them poor pigmentation in the eye-rims, nose, nails and lips. To breed to the truest colors, breeders must have an excellent understanding of the genetic color possibilities of the dogs to be bred.

Additionally, most Poodles are not the same color at birth as they are at maturity. In some cases, it takes more than a year for the color to "clear." Silver Poodles, for example, are usually born black and later fade to silver.

GAIT

How should a Poodle move? According to the breed standard, a Poodle's *gait is a straightforward trot with light springy action and strong hindquarters drive. Head and tail carried up. Sound, effortless movement is essential.*

TEMPERAMENT

The breed standard is concerned not only with the Poodle's physical characteristics but also with its temperament, or natural disposition.

The breed standard defines temperament as: *Carrying itself proudly, very active, intelligent, the Poodle has about itself an air of distinction and dignity peculiar to itself. Major fault: shyness or sharpness.*

Much can be said about the Poodle's temperament and personality. In fact, its good nature, intelligence and self-assured attitude are why the Poodle is, and has been, such a popular breed. Poodles are described as being "almost human," and they make excellent pets.

DISQUALIFICATIONS

According to the breed standard, Poodles may be disqualified for the following reasons:

Size: *A dog over or under the specified height limits shall be disqualified.*

Clip: *A dog in any type of clip other than those listed under "Coat" shall be disqualified.*

Parti-colors: *The coat of a parti-colored dog is not an even solid color at the skin but of two or more colors. Parti-colored dogs shall be disqualified.*

What about Poodles who fail to meet the standard set forth by the Poodle Club of America? Certainly, such dogs would not go far in the show ring and should not be bred and allowed to reproduce—at least not by a responsible breeder. Such dogs would be considered as pets, companion animals *not* to be bred. They are usually spayed or neutered, or shown in obedience.

Does a pet Poodle make a good family dog? Absolutely. The average dog owner has no business breeding anyway, considering the pet overpopulation problem. Leave breeding in the hands of experts. Even in the best kennels there are Poodles that do not make the grade as show champions. When this happens, the dog still has the wonderful future of a companion animal.

chapter 2

The Poodle's Ancestry

Poodles have been charming humans for generations. Images of Poodle-like dogs have been found carved on Roman tombs, suggesting that the breed is one of the oldest around today. There are many references to it in fifteenth- and sixteenth-century art and literature, and it is said to have been a favorite pet during the eighteenth century—and of King Louis XVI of France. Poodles have been known equally as entertainers: they were performers in Queen Anne's court in England and they have been circus stars.

Indeed, Poodles enjoy a long history, but tracing their origin is another matter. Much of what is known about yesteryear's Poodle is found in references in literature and art, so mapping a precise history is difficult at best.

From Whence They Came

Today's Poodle probably originated as a water retriever, and some speculate the breed could be the original Water Spaniel. In sixteenth-century Europe a dog called the Water Dog of England was quite popular among hunters. It was well suited for aquatic duties with its strong build, water-repellent coat and webbed feet. Some say today's Poodle is a direct descendant of the Water Dog; others believe the breeds merged. It is also believed that the Irish Water Spaniel descends from this same lineage. However, some theorize that the Irish Water Spaniel—which sports a curly coat similar to the Poodle and is an adept retriever—is the forerunner of the Poodle.

The Poodle is believed to have originated in Germany, though to name a specific country of origin is impossible. It is probably more accurate to state that the Poodle is a product of the entire European continent. Practically every European country has claimed the Poodle as its own, with Germany, Russia and France being the chief contenders.

It is interesting to note that Spain might be in a better position than most European countries to claim origination of the Poodle. This idea is based on the premise that the Poodle is part of the spaniel family, and the word *spaniel* is derived from the word *Spain*. This is where the spaniel developed, even if it did not originate there. It is not unreasonable to think that Spain might have had something to do with the very beginnings of what is now the Poodle breed. It has been stated that the Water Spaniel is one of the oldest breeds of dogs and that it was brought from the East, through Spain, to the British Isles. This is one of many possibilities of the Poodle's origin, but an interesting

**FAMOUS
OWNERS OF
POODLES**

Judy Garland

Tipper Gore

Helen Hayes

Carolina
Herrera

Sophia Loren

Edgar Allan
Poe

Sugar Ray
Robinson

Gertrude Stein

John Steinbeck

Tracey Ullman

one. In Spain today there is an ancient breed of dog used by fishermen to retrieve lost tackle. It resembles the Poodle and is called *Cao d' Agua*—Water Dog.

German writings from the sixteenth century describe the *Pudel*—a word that is derived from the verb *pudelin,* meaning "splashing in water"—as a fairly large, black, water retriever. In the 1600s, in some instances, this Water Dog was begun to be called a Pudel. In 1642, an incredible reference is made to a white Pudel called Boye who was credited with mystical powers that he used on behalf of his English master, Prince Rupert.

The dog was also found in Belgium and Holland as a working dog called *Poedel.* Most likely, the English name, Poodle, descends from these terms.

TRÉS FRANÇAIS

The French, however, have long claimed the Poodle as their own, hence the common name, "French Poodle." Indeed, the dogs found a devoted following in France. First known as the *Barbet* (a term that means "beard" and is used to describe any dog with long hair), and later as the *Caniche* (duck dog), the Poodle was a popular hunting dog. It also seems to have gained national recognition, although there doesn't seem to be irrefutable evidence to prove this idea. French literary references note a "vigorous, intelligent, sturdy, curly-haired dog that goes into the water," a description that matches the English Water Dog and the German

---

WHERE DID DOGS COME FROM?

It can be argued that dogs were right there at man's side from the beginning of time. As soon as human beings began to document their existence, the dog was among their drawings and inscriptions. Dogs were not just friends, they served a purpose: There were dogs to hunt birds, pull sleds, herd sheep, burrow after rats—even sit in laps! What your dog was originally bred to do influences the way it behaves. The American Kennel Club recognizes over 140 breeds, and there are hundreds more distinct breeds around the world. To make sense of the breeds, they are grouped according to their size or function. The AKC has seven groups:

1) Sporting, 2) Working,
3) Herding, 4) Hounds,
5) Terriers, 6) Toys,
7) Nonsporting

Can you name a breed from each group? Here's some help: (1) Golden Retriever; (2) Doberman Pinscher; (3) Collie; (4) Beagle; (5) Scottish Terrier; (6) Maltese; and (7) Dalmatian. All modern domestic dogs (*Canis familiaris*) are related, however different they look, and are all descended from *Canis lupus*, the gray wolf.

Pudel. Most likely, the name "French Poodle" can be attributed to its popularity in France.

The standard-size Poodle is believed to be the oldest among today's three sizes—Toy, Miniature and Standard. The larger Poodles were initially most common, but as Poodle fanciers grew interested in breeding for size, miniatures and toys appeared on the scene. Germans differentiated the Pudel into the *gross* (great), *mittlere* (medium) and *klein* (little). The term *Schaf* Pudel described dogs with woolly coats and the term *Schnurl* Pudel described dogs with corded coats.

CRYSTAL PALACE. OCT 19th 1899   *Champion Vladipeit* 611   STANDARD DATA 20 190" 3¾

The French distinguished among sizes, as well. General terms such as *grand* and *petit* Barbet differentiated large and small dogs, while the specific names of *Chiencanne* and *Caniche* were used to classify large and small duck dogs. The terms *Mouton* and *Moufflon* were used to describe a woolly or corded coat, respectively.

An early champion shows fine form.

Another, more widely accepted, theory is that Miniatures are the result of breeding small Standards. Likewise, the Toy is said to be the result of breeding small Miniatures.

The Miniature and Toy Poodles that have gained such popularity today have been standardized only within the last century. This is not to say that smaller-size Poodles did not exist in the early days of the breed; they did, as was mentioned above. In fact, a series of paintings by Bernadine Pinturiccio in 1490 featured Toy-size Poodles, and, also in the fifteenth century, the painter Frans Hals depicted a Toy attending a garden party. However, early small Poodles did not enjoy, or reflect, the benefits of breeding for a standard type as well as size.

Circus Dogs

The Poodle's reputation as a performer or circus animal can be traced to France. As early as 1700 the French discovered the natural, clownish talent of the breed. A troupe of Poodles from France, called Performing Dogs or Dancers, is said to have performed in London for King George III. Typical of these performing dogs were those of Signor M. Girmondi, who presented his dogs before the crowned heads of Europe in Berlin, Paris, Vienna and Madrid. The dogs pushed a wheelbarrow, danced, jumped through hoops, skipped rope, operated a spinning wheel and tumbled.

A combination advertisement, advance sheet and program, published in Manchester, England, in 1817, describes the act: "Their years are young but their experience old; and this description paints their tricks, which far transcend the power of pen to give. One scene is that of two dogs coming on stage bearing a sedan-chair in which is seated a tumbler who though not more than two months old is adept on ground and lofty exploits. This scene peculiarly claims the attention of the audience. After finished the tumbling he is carried off in the same vehicle. This young tumbler is a small French Poodle of great sagacity and quick apprehension, capable of being instructed in most tricks and receives his lessons with attention, particularly from one month old and upwards."

The Poodle became popular in England around 1800. English soldiers, engaged in the Napoleonic Wars on the Continent, were taken with the Pudel of Germany and the Caniche of France. The English soldiers found that a Poodle served as a mascot to practically every French regiment, and they brought home as many Poodles as they could.

Unfortunately, the Poodle was losing its reputation as a hardworking, intelligent, hardy hunting companion and instead was earning a reputation for being a trick dog or high-society pet. Sportsman T. Heath Joyce, one of the first enthusiasts of the Poodle in

England, complained that the Poodle was not appreciated as it should be: "and yet in great measure those very characteristics which render him first and foremost among canine performers are due to the simple fact that he is far superior in intelligence to his fellows, and capable of acquiring a greater variety of accomplishments, from walking about on his hind-legs with a parasol and petticoats, to retrieving on land or water."

A HISTORY OF HAIR

The elaborate coat styles of the Poodle undoubtedly enhanced the circus-like perception of the breed, but such styling can be traced to the early days of the breed. As was mentioned in the discussion of the Poodle's coat in Chapter 1, early dogs had heavy, water-repellent coats that helped keep them warm while dashing in and out of water. Those dense coats often hampered the dog's movement once wet. The solution was to trim the hair short on the hindquarters, leaving it full around the dog's chest for warmth. Later, "bobbles" were left on to protect the joints from rheumatism. The hair was also tied back from the eyes, first with a string and later with colored ribbon to make the dog more easily visible when swimming or in the field.

*Ch. Venda's
Gold Bell, 1941*

In 1654, veterinary writer Gervase Markham commented on hair trims in his book, *Hunger's Prevention, or The Art of Fowling*. The Water Dogs, he wrote, "are ever more laden with hair on the hinder parts and in the summertime by the violence of the heate is very noysome and troublesome, and make him sooner faint and give over his sport. So, likewise, in matter of water, it makes a very heavy burthen to the dogge and maketh him to swim less nimbly. Now for the cutting or shaving from the navell downwards, and backwards, is two ways well to be allowed; that is, for the summer hunting. But for the shaving of a dogge quite all over from foot to nostrill, that I utterly dislike, for it brings such a tendernesse and chillnesse over all his body that the water will grow irksome to him."

The clips accepted for show today are offshoots of this early practicality, but as time went on coat styling for the Poodle became more ornamental. Nineteenth-century France saw the rise of the business of Poodle grooming, when no style of clip seemed too outrageous; intricate designs and family crests were clipped into Poodle coats. The *New York Daily Tribune* commented on the stylish grooming of Poodles in 1893: "They are the favorites of the Parisian belles. Female poodle barbers are now an institution in Paris, for they make the Parisian poodles. They take a poodle and when they are through with him he is trimmed and decorated in the most elaborate and approved styles. These barbers cut off some of the hair, so that what is left is in the form of rosettes, bangs and other designs. The dog, after the artist barber is through with him, looks like a strange animal. The Parisian belle is different from the American girl, for instead of leaving her pet at home she takes him wherever she goes and has him decked in fancy costumes made of material to match her own gown. Sometimes the dogs are adorned with jewelled bangles and ribbons."

A Poodle from 1938

Another phenomenon at the time, and one that was considered quite fashionable, was the Corded Poodle. A Corded Poodle is one whose coat is rolled and twisted into long, tight ringlets. Each rope-like ringlet is formed individually, with the help of wax or petroleum jelly, and is left to grow until it reaches the ground. The cords were often tied up in linen to protect them. The Corded Poodle must have been quite a sight, but its popularity waned, probably due to the impracticality of keeping such a coat in condition.

In the late 1800s, when the Corded Poodle was at its peak in popularity, formal registration of the breed began. At early shows, Poodles were frequently corded, and a battle raged as to whether the Corded Poodle and the Curly (non-corded) were separate branches of the same family. Some claimed that the corded coat was the result of breeding unrelated to the non-corded dogs. But others refuted that idea and stated that any Poodle could be corded, if the coat was conditioned properly. The latter opinion is generally accepted today, and, if there ever were two different types of Poodles, the Corded Poodle has ceased to exist.

A Toy Poodle, 1939

The Poodle in the U.S.

The Poodle was introduced to the United States in the late 1800s, and the first Poodle was registered in the American Kennel Club Stud Book in 1887. It was not until a group of dedicated fanciers founded the Poodle Club of America in 1931, however, that the breed was generally noticed.

Early Poodles in the United States were imported, for the most part, from England. They were mostly black, white or brown, and the Standard size attracted the most interest. Poodle registration with the American Kennel Club was minimal and few were exhibited at shows. The largest number that was exhibited—thirty-four—during that time was in 1913 at the Westminster show in New York. Pet Poodles were found in homes, but they were far from popular dogs.

Both Standard and Toy Poodles were shown before the beginning of World War I, but they were considered separate breeds. As Miniatures became popular, they were shown with the Standards. In competition, how-

21

ever, they were divided into two coat types: curly and corded. The early Toys were considered a separate breed until 1943 when the American Kennel Club recognized them as the third variety of Poodle.

A few enthusiasts, most in the Northeast, worked toward wider acceptance and understanding of the breed, which was considered an object of curiosity rather than an intelligent, talented breed of dog. The newly established breed club set forth a breed standard by which American breeders defined the dog, based on the standard and rules of The Curley Poodle Club of England. These dedicated efforts on behalf of the Poodle paid off. In 1930 there were only thirty-four Poodles registered with the American Kennel Club; by 1960 there were more Poodles registered with the American Kennel Club than any other breed. In 1993, 67,850 were registered.

*Posing in
Greenwich, CT,
1938*

TODAY'S POODLE

The Poodle we know today comes in three sizes and myriad coat colors, and it is intelligent and a wonderful companion. But most of all, the Poodle's ancestry and history show the breed's versatility. From hunting companion, to circus entertainer, to family pet and show dog, the Poodle has the ability—and talent—to adapt to a variety of circumstances.

Is the Poodle still hunting? Yes, and those who employ its retrieving talents swear by them. The Poodle is a great showman and well able to bring home blue ribbons as a show dog. The Poodle does not just have good looks; it also performs well in obedience trials.

And, most important, the Poodle today is a popular, devoted companion to men, women and children.

chapter 3

The **World**
According to the
Poodle

Once you get to know the Poodle personality, it is not difficult to understand the dog's popularity throughout the ages. The Poodle is highly intelligent, active though not hyperactive, good natured and self-assured. It is a breed that carries itself with distinction, though many note that the Poodle has a sense of humor. The Poodle is adaptable, suited to a show career, life in the field or life as household pet—adaptability few

breeds can claim. Such positive qualities invite interest and appreciation, both of which the Poodle has enjoyed for generations.

23

The Poodle Is Versatile

Of these wonderful qualities, is there one that stands out? Again and again, breeders, enthusiasts, veterinarians—anyone who knows the Poodle—remark on the dog's almost human intelligence. It is one smart dog, they say, enamored by the breed's cognitive abilities.

For example, Poodles learn amazingly quickly; as long as their owners or trainers make the lesson understandable, the dogs will respond. The ability to learn, and do so eagerly, is what enables the Poodle to fulfill the various roles— retriever, performer, show dog—he has had throughout his history.

Poodles excel at obedience training, whether learning basic house manners or working toward a Utility title. In fact, the Poodle is the underlying force in bringing obedience training and showing to the United States. It began with a Poodle fancier in the early 1930s. Helene Whitehouse Walker imported three Standard Poodles from England and began breeding them under the Carillon name. She was an avid reader of English dog papers, which were reporting about ongoing obedience tests.

The Carillon Standards were shown in conformation competition, bringing in wins at Westminister. English Champion Whippendell Poli of Carillon won Best of Breed at the first Poodle Club of America show in 1933.

A DOG'S SENSES

Sight: With their eyes located farther apart than ours, dogs can detect movement at a greater distance than we can, but they can't see as well up close. They can also see better in less light, but can't distinguish many colors.

Sound: Dogs can hear about four times better than we can, and they can hear high-pitched sounds especially well. Their ancestors, the wolves, howled to let other wolves know where they were; our dogs do the same, but they have a wider range of vocalizations, including barks, whimpers, moans and whines.

Smell: A dog's nose is his greatest sensory organ. His sense of smell is so great he can follow a trail that's weeks old, detect odors diluted to one-millionth the concentration we'd need to notice them, even sniff out a person under water!

Taste: Dogs have fewer taste buds than we do, so they're likelier to try anything—and usually do, which is why it's especially important for their owners to monitor their food intake. Dogs are omnivores, which means they eat meat as well as vegetable matter like grasses and weeds.

Touch: Dogs are social animals and love to be petted, groomed and played with.

Soon, Walker began to develop obedience tests similar to those in England. The first all-breed obedience test was held at her father's estate in 1933. In 1934, Blanche Saunders, who later became Walker's associate, answered her advertisement for kennel help.

Together, the women pioneered the U.S. obedience movement, and their training guides and books remain important references today.

When the American Kennel Club took over responsibility for obedience competition, Walker and Saunders focused on increasing awareness of obedience training. The women traveled, with their dogs, equipment and training materials, throughout the United States. Their trip, and the early efforts of obedience in this country, are documented in Saunders's book, *The Story of Dog Obedience.*

Poodles make great playmates.

In 1935, the first AKC-licensed obedience trials were held by the Obedience Test Club of New York. By August of that year, twelve Poodles had completed the requirements for the "Companion Dog" title.

As bright as the breed is, the Poodle has been the victim of misperception. Considered too "fancy" or "frilly," particularly by men, the amazing intellect of the Poodle has been overlooked. And, perhaps understandably, some perception of the breed is linked to its unusual coat and trimmings. The hair styles are often perceived as frivolous. Don't be fooled by elaborate coat patterns, though. What is underneath all the fluff and puffs is anything but frivolous. Awaiting is a keen mind, ready and able to accomplish most any task.

Not only is the Poodle intelligent, she is also highly adaptable. She fits into the lifestyle and tempo of

any household very well, whether the home be in the
city or country, with or without children or other pets,
and the family small or large. In addition to her easy
personality, the Poodle also comes in three sizes.
Owners can select a size that best fits their lifestyles and
budgets.

The Poodle's flexibility even extends to how he relates
to his owner. You will find little personality conflict
with your Poodle because the Poodle adapts his personality to his owner. He is very sensitive to his owner,
which is perhaps the result of his heritage as a hunting
companion eagerly awaiting direction.

The Poodle is often described as an active dog, though
not hyperactive. She enjoys working as a retriever,
being part of family activities, making a round in the
show ring or just taking a walk through the neighborhood. And, in most cases, the Poodle works with tail-
wagging exuberance.

Thick-headed and stubborn this breed is not. Rather,

the Poodle is sensitive
and, as mentioned pre-
viously, learns quickly.
He has a unique ability
to read situations and
clues and respond ap-
propriately. Once the
dog knows and under-
stands what is expected,
he will comply happily.
The Poodle is extremely
eager to please his owner.

*A tiny Toy
waits to be
carried off to
the picnic.*

As noted in the Official
Standard for the Poodle, the Poodle has an air of
distinction and dignity peculiar to herself. Such
characteristics are difficult to measure since they are
subjective and open to interpretation; they could be
considered anthropomorphic (attributing human
characteristics to an animal) by some.

Those who understand and live with the breed, however, are quick to describe this aspect of the Poodle's personality. The breed is known as neat, noble and stately. This is reflected in the way the Poodle carries himself and relates to people and his environment, most often with a head-up, tail-up attitude. Attend a dog show and watch a champion Poodle trot for the

judge or stand for examination. "Dignified" is the adjective that will certainly come to mind.

Contrasting the Poodle's air of dignity is its playful, fun-loving streak. Described as a "sense of humor" by those who know and love the breed, the Poodle is well able to amuse owners

A Toy Poodle does a retrieve over the hurdle.

with her antics. The ability to make people laugh, to perform, to suddenly break out of a "sophisticated" air, is probably why the breed excelled as a circus and stage performer.

The fun side of the Poodle's personality is illustrated clearly in the following story by *Your Poodle* author Frank T. Sabella about the legendary International Champion Nunsoe Duc de la Terrace of Blakeen. (The story was orginally told in Hayes Blake Hoyt's *Saga of Duc*.)

Duc was born and brought up in Switzerland, lived part of his life in France and then England, and was brought to America by Mrs. Hoyt in 1933. He had outstanding success as a show dog in all these countries, and he was the first Poodle to win the most publicized dog show in the United States, that of the Westminster Kennel Club in New York City. His beauty and showmanship had much to do with winning the hearts and understanding of the American public when Poodles were not popular in this country.

Mrs. Hoyt gives us our first picture of Duc as she waited at the dock for his arrival by boat from England. An awestruck and admiring crowd seperates to reveal a "superb white creature," dazzling and majestic, calm and totally aloof to the confusion and activity around him.

It is the Duc.

He was standing at the end of a lead held by the ship's butcher. Then he walked assuredly down the gangplank; a large, beautifully made dog, noble visitor to our land, which was to become his own. And as the butcher handed over the lead, he said, "You are lucky. This dog's different. He ain't a dog—he's human."

CHARACTERISTICS OF THE POODLE

Highly intelligent

Good natured

Suitable to a show career or life as a companion pet

Excellent at obedience training

Self-assured

Dignified

Active and energetic

It seems that Duc was well mannered, but reserved, with his new owner for several days after he reached his home in the United States. Then suddenly one afternoon he took a hat from a chair, "eyes blazing with mischief," and dashed out onto the lawn implying that a chase was in order. He was finally at home. He had accepted his new mistress as his own. And as Mrs. Hoyt said, "We learned that we had a clown as well as king."

Duc proved himself a clown one evening at a "pompous" dinner party. He had been left upstairs, in case some of the guests did not like dogs; one senses that he may have been somewhat provoked by this slight. Meanwhile, at dinner, the subject of the famous white Poodle was raised; just as his owner was about to expound on his greatness, in walked Duc, all dignity and elegance—with an enema bag in his mouth! As if in the show ring, he marched around the table and out of the room, tail wagging.

Comparing the Sizes

A wonderful aspect of the Poodle is that it comes in three sizes, a sort of three-sizes-fits-all breed. Although the breed standard, excluding size, is the same for all three varieties, is it really the same dog?

For the most part, yes. Poodles of all sizes are intelligent, adaptable and energetic. There are some differences to be aware of that can affect which variety one might choose. The differences are not really differences in the essence of the breed, but are rather by-products of the particular size.

Of course, there are enthusiasts for each size. Some will recommend the Standard Poodle over other sizes; others tout the wonders found in a Toy package. Still others advocate the blessings of the Miniature. In the end, though, all three varieties are wonderful dogs. No size is a bad choice.

The Toy is probably the most pampered of all the sizes.

The *Toy* is considered highly portable, which contributes to its popularity. These dogs travel well, space requirements are limited and, in spite of their small size, they are strong in spirit. The Toy has been described as a small version of the Standard; she obviously is not capable of retrieving game and the like, however, even though she may think she can.

Unfortunately, perhaps because of their small, toy-like appearance, many owner tend to spoil this variety. Size is no reason to disregard manners, though. Basic obedience training is essential for any Poodle.

Should families with children consider a Toy? Some believe that the larger Poodles are better able to handle the day-to-day roughhousing that may occur with children. Certainly, responsible children, supervised by an adult, can be trusted with the diminutive Toy.

The *Miniature* Poodle is also portable. It is a larger dog than the Toy, but it does not have the larger space requirements of the Standard. The Miniature is an ideal middle-of-the-road choice.

A Standard playing in the snow of Montana.

Enthusiasts say there is nothing like a *Standard*—and that is certainly true. But keep in mind that Standards are big dogs, requiring proper accommodations and exercise. This is not to say that a Standard cannot live happily in an apartment. As long as the owner is committed to daily walks and romps in the park, and does not intend to leave the dog alone day and evening, he will be fine. It is not so much the environment but what the owner is willing to provide that is important.

Grooming is essential for any size Poodle, and the bigger the Poodle, the bigger, and more expensive, the grooming job. The differences among the varieties just in brushing time is considerable. Multiply that by bathing, drying, clipping and scissoring—it adds up quickly.

The Poodle accepts the necessities of grooming very well, which is fortunate considering the amount required to keep a coat in good shape, whether she be pet or show dog. Professional groomers can attest to Poodles' cooperative spirits. Poodles are often favorite customers because they can be taught to sit or stand quietly for brushing or scissoring, hold a paw up for clipping or peacefully tolerate ear cleaning. The Poodle is often the easiest dog to groom, despite her thick coat or complicated trim, because she is so willing to comply. In fact, Poodles seem to enjoy being groomed, as though they appreciate the importance of a neat and tidy appearance.

Grooming should begin right away—as early as six weeks—to accustom the youngster to the routine.

Some breeders begin clipping faces and feet as early as three weeks. Poodle puppies adjust to brushing, the sound of electric clippers and warm air from a blow dryer quickly, once they learn what these activities mean. It is rare for a Poodle to fight continually against the grooming process, although individual dogs may mildly object to certain procedures, such as toenail clipping. For the most part, expect a Poodle, regardless of size, to accept—downright enjoy—grooming. See Chapter 6, *Grooming Your Poodle,* for detailed information on grooming.

MORE INFORMATION ON POODLES

National Breed Club

Poodle Club of America, Inc.
Charles Thomasson, Corresponding Secretary
503 Martineau Drive
Chester, VA 23831-5753

The club can give you information on all aspects of the breed, including the names and addresses of breed and obedience clubs in your area. Inquire about membership.

BOOKS

Cherry, Barbara. *The Pet Owner's Guide to the Poodle.* New York: Howell Book House, 1994.

Dahl, Del. *The Complete Poodle.* New York: Howell Book House, 1994.

Irick, Mackey J. *The New Poodle.* New York: Howell Book House, 1986.

Nicholas, Anna Katherine. *The Book of the Poodle.* Neptune, N.J.: TFH Publications, 1984.

Nicholas, Anna Katherine. *Poodles: A Complete Introduction.* Neptune, N.J.: TFH Publications, 1985

Sabella, Frank T. *Your Poodle, Standard, Miniature and Toy.* Middleburg, Va.: William W. Denlinger, 1969.

Tracy, T.H. *The Book of the Poodle.* New York: The Viking Press, 1950.

Ullmann, H.J. and Ullmann, E. *Poodles.* Hauppauge, N.Y.: Barron's Educational Series, 1987.

Magazines

Poodle Review. Hoflin Publishing, Inc. 4401 Zephyr Street, Wheat Ridge, CO 80033-3299.

Videos

The American Kennel Club. *Poodles.*

Living

with a

part two

Poodle

chapter 4

Bringing your
Poodle
Home

The temptation to buy or adopt a Poodle puppy impulsively can be overwhelming. Puppies are cute, especially Poodles, no matter what size. Too often, though, owners bring home a puppy or dog without giving it much thought and, well, the rest of the story is not necessarily happily ever after. Why is that?

It is because dogs—puppies and adults—have a variety of needs that owners are not always prepared to meet. Or a new owner does not really understand the basics of proper dog care.

To make both a Poodle puppy's arrival in a new home and life thereafter a happy one, owners must be prepared. Following are some basics to think about *before* bringing a puppy or adult Poodle home.

Commitment and Responsibility

On average, dogs live about twelve years. That means that once the cute Poodle puppy crosses the threshold, the owner is, for the next twelve years or so, responsible for its daily care. This entails daily walks, feeding and brushing; weekly bed washing and trips to the pet supply store; monthly visits to the groomer; biannual veterinary checkups; and so on. Vacations must be planned in advance with accommodations—a kennel stay or a housesitter—for the dog. Costly medical emergencies can arise, as well.

The Poodle is also dependent upon its owner for companionship and training. The dog's behavior, good or bad, reflects an owner's efforts and understanding of the *Canis familiaris* species.

But do not be discouraged by all this. *Be realistic.* An owner who is not willing, or able, to provide properly for a Poodle, for its entire life, will cause unnecessary suffering for the dog. It is better to "just say no" to adopting a pet if commitment and responsibility are lacking, or if funds are limited. However, if you are willing to take on the challenge of daily caring for, and nurturing, a Poodle, you will reap a bountiful harvest.

Remember, what a Poodle or any pet needs most is a committed, responsible owner.

CHANGE IN LIFESTYLE— THE FIRST YEAR

With the adoption of a Poodle puppy or adult comes a change in lifestyle—your lifestyle. Dogs have special needs, at each stage of growth, and they are dependent upon their owners to fulfill them.

Puppies are especially demanding, with their short attention spans, curiosity, bursts of playfulness, teething troubles and lack of socialization and training. Training, caring and meeting such needs will undoubtedly warrant change in an owner's lifestyle.

PUPPY ESSENTIALS

Your new puppy will need:

food bowl

water bowl

collar

leash

I.D. tag

bed

crate

toys

grooming supplies

The Poodle's most impressionable period is between six weeks and six months. During this time, a pup develops its social skills and attitudes toward life. Pups that are well socialized and exposed to a wide variety of situations grow up to be well-adjusted adults. Pups that play with other puppies develop a good attitude toward other dogs, which helps prevent aggressive tendencies and shyness in the adult dog. Pups that are handled lovingly by people will develop trust toward people in general.

Most puppies will demonstrate mouthing or biting behavior. If this happens during teething periods, usually around four months, a chew toy is essential. Chewing behavior will cease as the puppy matures, but bad habits can develop. Teach youngsters to chew only acceptable items.

Puppies commonly urinate when they are excited or frightened. This is not a voluntary act and should not be punished. When a youngster urinates in this manner, it is acknowledging the superiority of others present, dogs or people. This usually dissipates as the dog matures.

Accustom your puppy to riding in a car early. Many puppies experience car sickness on their first rides. Minimize this by withholding food before traveling, and start with short trips. For the dog's safety, confine him in a crate or specially designed car restraint when traveling. Do not allow a dog to ride in the open back of a truck or hang his head out the window while driving.

PUPPY-PROOFING

The big day has arrived: It is time to bring home your Poodle. Not much to think about, right?

Wrong.

Like young children, puppies, even some adult dogs, are curious and mischievous, and they have a tendency to put anything and everything in their mouths. Just as parents might child-proof a home to make it safer for a youngster, Poodle owners should puppy-proof their homes and yards to ensure the animal's safety.

Begin in the kitchen, because it can be such an enticing place and you tend to spend a lot of time there. Take a close look around. Are electrical cords from appliances within reach? How about breakable items that could be tugged off a counter? Store any such items well out of reach. The aroma of discarded leftovers can cause even a good dog to go bad, so be sure the garbage pail has a lid or is stored out of your Poodle's reach. Cleaning supplies are essential, especially when you own dogs. Be sure your Poodle never has access to these products, though. Consider placing safety locks on all cabinets.

Puppies are in endless need of your time and affection.

Check the bathroom carefully. Store all drugs and other medicine-chest items to prevent accidental poisoning. Keep toilet bowl lids down to prevent the Poodle from drinking out of the bowl and possibly ingesting toilet bowl cleaners or other products.

Is the living room decorated with luscious green plants? Plants add life and warmth to a room, but they can be harmful to the Poodle who ingests them. Find out which plants are pet-safe before decorating.

Are cords to the television, VCR or stereo neatly coiled and stored so the dog will not be tempted to play with them? Too often pets chew on electric cords with shocking results.

The garage is often a deadly place for pets because it is a common area to store toxic chemicals such as snail bait, antifreeze or paint. If this is the case, it is probably best to store such products out of reach and to prohibit the dog from entering the garage.

The yard or kennel area must be safe, too. Make sure all fencing is secure and free of sharp edges. Do not store equipment, landscaping tools and so forth in a yard designated for the dog. Remember that anything placed in the yard is likely to be investigated.

HOUSEHOLD DANGERS

Curious puppies and inquisitive dogs get into trouble not because they are bad, but simply because they want to investigate the world around them. It's our job to protect our dogs from harmful substances, like the following:

IN THE HOUSE

cleaners, especially pine oil

perfumes, colognes, aftershaves

medications, vitamins

office and craft supplies

electric cords

chicken or turkey bones

chocolate

some house and garden plants, like ivy, oleander and poinsettia

IN THE GARAGE

antifreeze

garden supplies, like snail and slug bait, pesticides, fertilizers, mouse and rat poisons

A Dog's Second Best Friend

Today, veterinary medicine can provide pets with treatments that might have been considered miracles a few years ago. To ensure the Poodle's health and well-being, take advantage of new knowledge and technology by teaming up with a veterinarian, even before acquiring your dog. By doing so, your Poodle will be healthier and you will learn more about caring for your pet.

The benefits of regular visits to the veterinarian do not stop there. Routine visits build trust, understanding and respect between the vet and the Poodle owner. Should an emergency or difficult situation arise, the good rapport between client and vet can make all the difference.

Basic Supplies

There is a certain amount of basic equipment and supplies that goes along with owning a dog. This means a trip to a pet supply store is in order before bringing home the new Poodle.

First, determine where, and in or on what, the dog will sleep. It is a good idea to assign one specific location to the dog, a "den" of sorts, to give it a sense of security. Bedding can be as simple as a blanket tossed on the floor or as elaborate as a wicker basket with a five-inch-thick colorful print cushion. It can also be a crate, an enclosed cage with a door that is commonly used for transporting dogs on airlines. A crate is a good choice if a specific room, such as a laundry room, is not available to designate to the dog.

Now that the Poodle's bedding is squared away, consider feeding dishes. There are bowls designed to keep ants out, bowls that sit in a stand and bowls made of stainless steel. Some bowls are plastic; others are earthenware. There are light bowls and heavy bowls. A case can be made for any one of these, but it is probably best to start simply. Ask your breeder, veterinarian or a fellow Poodle owner for a suggestion. Then select two bowls, one for food and one for water, and choose a size that best fits your Poodle's size.

Naturally, those bowls must be filled, so include dog food on the shopping list. Ask the breeder what he or she has been feeding the puppy or dog. Ask for a sample or purchase the same kind, or ask a veterinarian for a recommendation. Do not be tempted to make a radical switch because this can cause digestive upset. Change foods gradually over several days, mixing in the new food with the old diet.

A collar and leash are in order. Once again, owners will find an amazing array of sizes, types and styles on the market. There are leather collars and leashes; nylon; rolled or flat collars; harnesses; colorful or plain. Style is an individual choice; just make sure to attach an identification tag with a current name, address and telephone number to the collar. A second "choke" or training collar may be a good idea as well. These collars are meant to be worn only during supervised training sessions, though. Never leave a training collar on a dog because it could catch on something and the dog could choke to death.

Considering the Poodle's love of play, toys are essential. Young, teething puppies especially need safe chew toys; adult dogs may be happier with a rubber ball or pull ring, though many adult dogs still enjoy a good chew. Beware of toys with small parts.

41

It may take a few purchases before discovering the Poodle's favorite toy—and most dogs do have a favorite. Just make sure that favorite toy is safe!

Routine grooming is a *must* for every Poodle, regardless of size, so add grooming supplies and equipment to the shopping list. Purchase a brush and comb; shampoo, conditioner and some type of flea-control product; nail trimmers; and ear powder and cleaner.

Additional miscellaneous items include reference materials such as magazines and books about dogs and/or Poodles, carpet stain and odor remover, a "poop scoop" and a "baby" gate.

Start your Poodle on a grooming routine early and you will reap the benefits.

Exercise

To keep healthy, every Poodle needs exercise. How much and what type depends upon the variety of Poodle. The obviously smaller Toy does not have the same requirements as the Standard. Owners must take the Poodle's size into consideration when planning a fitness schedule.

The goal, no matter what size, is a properly conditioned dog, one that is an appropriate weight—neither too heavy nor too thin—and that is muscular and energetic.

A fitness routine can be as simple as a brisk walk around the neighborhood or an intense game of fetch in the park. Whatever the choice, make sure it is consistent—daily is best—and begin slowly. Just as people should begin a new fitness program slowly, so should dogs.

Obedience training is an excellent way to get a dog and owner active. Obedience training requires not only the Poodle's careful thought, but it also requires the dog to move.

chapter 5

Feeding
your
Poodle

Food. It's the fuel the Poodle needs to nourish his body, which in turn produces that special kind of Poodle energy owners so appreciate and enjoy. If the Poodle stops eating, or eats improperly, he suffers.

The domestic dog requires some 45 to 50 different nutrients in her diet. A deficiency of any one of those nutrients can cause illness. And each nutrient must be present in optimum ratios to each other for optimum health. If this balance is upset, from either lack of food or the wrong food, health problems can arise.

To prevent any such problems, an owner must make sure the Poodle eats properly and takes in the appropriate balance of nutrients.

Easier said than done, right? How can an owner possibly make sure her Poodle is receiving all those nutrients, especially when it is not clear what they all are?

Well, thanks to commercially prepared foods, owners need not scientifically calculate and formulate a pet's meal. Feeding a nutritionally balanced diet can be as easy—and complete—as opening a bag or can of food. Such foods have been prepared by companies dedicated to understanding the nutritional needs of dogs.

Nutrition

Protein: The Poodle relies on specific nutrients for its vigorous health and spectacular haircoat. Proteins, which are composed of amino acids found in meats, eggs, fish and soybeans, supply dogs with nutrients needed for growth, tissue repair and maintenance. They also form antibodies to fight infection.

Carbohydrates: Carbohydrates are the Poodle's energy sources. The dog's body uses carbohydrates for quick energy, thus sparing protein for body growth and repair. Cellulose, an indigestible carbohydrate, provides bulk for proper intestinal function.

Fats: Fats provide the Poodle with the most concentrated source of energy. They carry fat-soluble vitamins—D, E, A and K—and supply linoleic acid, a fatty acid that is important for skin and hair.

Vitamins and minerals: Vitamins and minerals are essential for normal body functions and bone development, as well as for certain chemical reactions in the body. The right balance of minerals is essential to the Poodle's health. For example, zinc is a trace mineral required for normal metabolism, including hair growth and skin health. A deficiency of zinc in a dog's diet can cause thinning hair and crusty dermatitis. And a deficiency of essential fatty acids can retard growth and produce coarse hair and dry, flaking skin.

Water: Last, but by no means least, is water. Dogs need a constant supply of fresh, clean water.

SELECTING FOOD

How do owners know which food best provides the above nutrients? Regardless of manufacturers' claims, there is no one right food for the Poodle. Finding the best diet for an individual dog may take some detective work. Ask the breeder for a recommendation. An experienced breeder usually has experimented with a number of brands of food, knows which foods agree with his or her Poodles and can give an unbiased opinion. Ask a veterinarian or pet supply retailer for a suggestion. Ask other Poodle owners for ideas. Then pick one and give it a try.

A good way to evaluate how a specific food agrees with your Poodle is to evaluate the feces on a regular basis. While certainly not a pleasant task, it is important. The feces can give clues to what is going on in the Poodle's gastrointestinal system. Most healthy dogs leave well-formed, firm droppings that emit little odor. Diarrhea is obviously a sign of illness, as is any other sudden change in the feces consistency. Such changes can also indicate a poor diet.

Feces consistency indicates how well an animal absorbs nutrients from the food, thus illustrating the balance of fiber and water and the all-around quality of the diet. Firm, proportional feces usually mean that the dog is receiving a high-quality diet formulated to enable the system to absorb as much of the nutrients as possible.

A high-quality dog food may be digested more quickly than one of poorer quality. The more quickly the food is digested, the less odor there will be in the feces. In

---

HOW MANY MEALS A DAY?

Individual dogs vary in how much they should eat to maintain a desired body weight—not too fat, but not too thin. Puppies need several meals a day, while older dogs may need only one. Determine how much food keeps your adult dog looking and feeling her best. Then decide how many meals you want to feed with that amount. Like us, most dogs love to eat, and offering two meals a day is more enjoyable for them. If you're worried about overfeeding, make sure you measure correctly and abstain from adding tidbits to the meals.

Whether you feed one or two meals, only leave your dog's food out for the amount of time it takes her to eat it—10 minutes, for example. Freefeeding (when food is available any time) and leisurely meals encourage picky eating. Don't worry if your dog doesn't finish all her dinner in the allotted time. She'll learn she should.

addition, feces that are an unusual color, such as green or magenta, may reflect coloring additives in the food.

Once a diet is selected and your Poodle seems to like it, stick with it. There is really no reason to switch, and doing so can cause problems. Complete diets are manufactured based on extensive research. Arbitrarily changing diets could create a nutritional imbalance.

TYPES OF FOOD

There are three basic types of commercial dog food: dry, canned and semimoist. Which one is best for the Poodle?

Opinions vary among manufacturers, vets, breeders and pet owners as to which type is best. Some believe in a dry-only diet, some feed canned only and there are those who mix canned or semimoist with dry. Or feed semimoist only. For the most part, all diets have their advantages.

One of the biggest differences between dry and canned foods is moisture content. Obviously, the moisture content in canned food is higher: 70 to 80 percent. Dry food is around 10 percent. Canned food is usually manufactured from fresh meat products, which accounts for the added moisture.

This higher moisture content has both an advantage and disadvantage. It is very appealing to dogs, but it is more expensive than the other varieties. The price per ounce

---

HOW TO READ THE DOG FOOD LABEL

With so many choices on the market, how can you be sure you are feeding the right food for your dog? The information is all there on the label—if you know what you're looking for.

Look for the nutritional claim right up top. Is the food "100% nutritionally complete"? If so, it's for nearly all life stages; "growth and maintenance," on the other hand, is for early development; puppy foods are marked as such, as are foods for senior dogs.

Ingredients are listed in descending order by weight. The first three or four ingredients will tell you the bulk of what the food contains. Look for the highest-quality ingredients, like meats and grains, to be among them.

The Guaranteed Analysis tells you what levels of protein, fat, fiber and moisture are in the food, in that order. While these numbers are meaningful, they won't tell you much about the quality of the food. Nutritional value is in the dry matter, not the moisture content.

In many ways, seeing is believing. If your dog has bright eyes, a shiny coat, a good appetite and a good energy level, chances are his diet's fine. Your dog's breeder and your veterinarian are good sources of advice if you're still confused.

of dry and canned food is about the same, but owners must feed three times as much canned food to meet caloric requirements. For large breeds, the costs can be prohibitive. Some say canned food is more digestible and that it has a longer shelf life, because cans are sealed air-tight.

A complete and balanced dry food is usually the most economical. It also helps eliminate tartar build-up on the dog's teeth and gums. Dry food must be stored properly to ensure its nutritional value, and the shelf life is an estimated twelve months. Most dry foods contain approved chemical preservatives such as BHA, BHT and ethoxyquin.

Dry food can seem boring to owners, which accounts for the practice of mixing a small portion of canned with dry food. Feeding a dry diet by itself, as long as the diet is "complete and balanced," is perfectly sufficient.

In between dry and canned foods are semimoist diets. These processed diets are usually packaged conveniently, eliminating the mess of canned food or the bulk of a 25-pound bag. Costs fall between canned and dry food, but shelf life is somewhat less than either.

It is best to avoid diets with high amounts of sugar, dyes or preservatives. For the holistic-minded, there are pet diets marketed as "natural" or "preservative-free."

Today, Poodles enjoy the benefits of diets made specifically for differing stages in life: puppy diets, adult diets and diets for seniors. Such diets are made with the dog's specific caloric needs in mind. There are also special diets made for dogs with health problems. Ask your veterinarian if a special diet is appropriate for your Poodle before feeding one.

Can owners make their own dog food? The best answer to that question is another: Why? With myriad good diets on the market, which are nutritionally complete for the dog, there is little benefit in "making" a dog's rations. Commericial diets are the product of years of research and experience. It is unlikely that an owner can match that in one afternoon in the kitchen.

It is important to note that there are times when a special, homemade diet is in order, most often following a veterinarian's recommendation. Other than when directed by a vet, Poodle owners should feed a balanced commercial diet, relax and enjoy the benefits of modern advances.

The type of diet the Poodle eats is less important than how well she fares on a particular food. If the dog is

alert, happy, with bright eyes, a shiny coat and no diarrhea, and she likes and eats the food, it is a safe bet the diet is the right choice.

How Much?

Generally, the Poodle's daily caloric requirements are:

If your Poodle eats all of her food at meal time and seems to be healthy, chances are you are feeding properly.

- Puppy: 100 calories per pound of body weight
- Adult: 60 calories per pound of body weight
- Geriatric: 25 calories per pound of body weight

This can vary among individual dogs depending upon size, activity, temperament, environment and metabolism. For example, a working dog that lives outside in a cold climate has greater caloric needs than an apartment-dwelling pet. Pregnancy, lactation and illness can also affect the dog's caloric needs. On the average, the Standard weighs 45 to 60 pounds; the Miniature weighs 14 to 17 pounds; and the Toy a mere five to seven pounds.

Given that weight can vary, you should examine your dog to see if the body fat is in correct proportion to height and bone. There should be a layer of subcutaneous fat over the ribs, thick enough to provide some padding and insulation, but not too thick. Individual ribs should be evident to the touch.

Weigh your Poodle periodically, especially if obesity is a problem. To do so, stand on a scale without your dog and calculate your weight. Then pick up your dog and step on the scale. Subtract your individual weight from the combined weight. The difference is your dog's weight.

How much should you feed your Poodle? Figure out your dog's weight and take into consideration his general caloric requirements per pound of body weight at his stage in life. Compare that to the type of food. Canned, dry and semimoist foods differ in calories per specific measurement. Read the label to determine how much food—one cup, one can and so forth—is required for a certain amount of calories. Then measure and feed.

If a diet change is in order, be sure to do it gradually, over a period of several days. Otherwise, the Poodle may develop diarrhea or other digestive upset. Begin by adding a small portion of new food to the regular diet. Increase the amount daily. Watch for signs of trouble, especially diarrhea. If this happens, call your veterinarian.

> **TO SUPPLEMENT OR NOT TO SUPPLEMENT?**
>
> If you're feeding your dog a diet that's correct for her developmental stage and she's alert, healthy-looking and neither over- nor underweight, you don't need to add supplements. These include table scraps as well as vitamins and minerals. In fact, a growing puppy is in danger of developing musculoskeletal disorders by oversupplementation. If you have any concerns about the nutritional quality of the food you're feeding, discuss them with your veterinarian.

FEEDING FREQUENCY

How often the Poodle needs to eat varies throughout its life, and varies among individual dogs.

Young puppies need to eat frequently. Generally, you should feed them four times daily at six to eight weeks of age, and three times daily by ten to twelve weeks. Once the puppy reaches sixteen weeks (four months) twice a day is sufficient. As the puppy becomes less interested in finishing a meal or becomes overweight, eliminate a feeding. At one year of age, one feeding a day is adequate. Breaking up the dog's daily allotment into two feedings, however, is generally more pleasant for the dog.

Some owners "freefeed," which means they fill up the bowl and leave it out. This is *not* recommended because it sends the message that the dog can eat at any time.

OBESITY

There is a great temptation for owners of all varieties of Poodles to overfeed. Overfeeding and obesity go hand in hand, however. Unfortunately, it is the dog that suffers: An overweight dog is uncomfortable, lethargic and prone to heart disease and other illnesses.

Make a vow not to overfeed your Poodle. Do not feed table scraps or excess treats, and make sure the dog gets enough exercise. If the dog is a finicky eater—and many of the smaller Poodles are, by their owner's making—don't be swayed by her refusal to eat. Offer a well-balanced diet, not a plate of leftovers. The dog may eat the leftovers, but she learns not to accept the appropriate food. As well, she is robbed of the proper balance of nutrients so essential to her health.

There is nothing wrong with treats, but do not feed them in place of a balanced diet. Offer treats only if the dog eats his regular meal and he is not overweight. Many owners feed their dogs bits of fresh vegetables as treats, which are inexpensive and low in calories.

Often, the bad habit of begging accompanies obesity. Discourage this bad habit; don't allow it. Place the dog in another room, in his crate or in the back yard during mealtime if necessary.

Foods to Avoid

Chocolate, with a chemical ingredient called *theobromine*, can cause severe digestive upset and even death. Keep all chocolate, especially that used for baking, which has the highest amount of theobromine, away from the dog. Do not leave a box of holiday candy sitting on the coffee table. A curious Poodle could help herself and end up very ill.

Rich foods, such as turkey skin, gravy and mashed potatoes, are popular around the holiday season, but don't allow your dog to indulge in them. The high fat content of such food will cause digestive upset.

Spicy foods are a no-no for the Poodle as well. Owners may enjoy the mouth-burning taste of chili peppers, but the Poodle will not. Spicy foods can cause digestive upset. Don't add raw eggs to the dog's food, either. Raw eggs can contain the potentially deadly bacteria, salmonella.

Keep your Poodle's weight in check.

Bones

Dogs love to chew bones, but not all bones are safe for dogs to chew. Avoid giving the Poodle turkey, chicken or pork bones—those that can splinter and end up causing intestinal damage. Large, hard and round bones, such as knuckle or marrowbones, are better choices. Parboil the bone to kill bacteria before offering it to your dog. Make sure the dog only chews the bone, though. Take it away if he begins to eat it.

Better yet, purchase chew toys. There are many safe and well-made synthetic bones on the market that will satisfy the dog's urge to chew.

chapter 6

Grooming
your
Poodle

The Poodle's wonderful temperament has a purpose. This good-natured dog makes an excellent friend for adults and children, a top hunting companion and incredible showman. But what may be of greater importance is that the Poodle really enjoys grooming.

This is important, considering the amount of grooming it takes to keep a Poodle looking good. Poodles are blessed with spectacular coats. A freshly bathed, fluffed and trimmed Poodle, whether pet or show dog, is a beautiful sight to behold.

Poodle grooming is an art form, and it requires skill, talent, patience, equipment and know-how. This is not to suggest that owners cannot learn to trim their own Poodles. They can. The reality is, however, that most owners do not learn the skill; instead, they ask a professional groomer to do the job.

Of course, owners must pay groomers for such services—again and again and again. Pet Poodles require full grooming—bath, fluff dry and hair cut—*at least* every six to eight weeks. In between visits, Poodles must be brushed and sometimes bathed, ears and teeth must be checked weekly and toenails may need to be trimmed or filed.

Poodles are high-maintenance dogs, though they are well worth the effort. Be realistic when assessing the Poodle's grooming requirements. This breed requires an owner who will commit to the never-ending cycle of bathing, brushing and trimming—and who will stick to it.

The grooming information here is geared to what owners can do for their pet Poodles at home.

SELECTING A BRUSH

Brushing and combing are the foundations of good grooming. It is essential to master these skills. Neglect brushing and combing, and your Poodle will look like a tattered coat.

Brushing is essential not only to keep the coat tangle-free, but also to distribute oils, increase skin circulation and remove dirt and dead skin. Increased circulation promotes healthy skin and hair regrowth. When you brush your Poodle, both his looks and the health of his skin improve.

The type of brush you use depends on the dog's coat and whether it is being groomed for show or home. The best is a wire slicker or pin brush. The wire slicker is excellent for brushing the thick, dense parts of the coat and for brushing out tangles. A pin brush is less effective on tangled coats, but it is excellent for the Poodle's long, silky ears and other long parts of the coat. Used properly, a pin brush will not tear or damage the coat as much as a slicker brush.

GROOMING TOOLS

pin brush

slicker brush

flea comb

towel

matt rake

grooming glove

scissors

nail clippers

tooth-cleaning equipment

shampoo

conditioner

clippers

Opinions do vary among groomers and Poodle breeders as to which brush is best. Ask your dog's breeder or a groomer what type of brush he or she uses. Then give it a try. If it is an effective tool, great. If not, try a different brush.

TECHNIQUE

Where do you begin once you have selected a brush? Assuming that the Poodle is well-mannered and familiar with the grooming process, place her on the grooming table. If a grooming table is not available, try the kitchen counter, washing machine, picnic table or any location that is waist-high and easy to clean. Be sure to place a rubber mat beneath the dog on slippery surfaces such as a countertop. You should groom the Poodle in this selected spot each time. That way, the dog will know what to expect at each grooming session.

Brush systematically, even if your dog has a short trim.

Brushing, and the entire grooming process, should be a systematic procedure. Many professional groomers begin brushing the dog's hindquarters, move to hind legs, tail, front legs, body, and finally the head and ears. When brushing is done systematically, it takes less time to brush the coat completely. The important idea is to develop a brushing pattern and use it each time.

A thorough brushing must precede bathing. This is especially important if the coat is long and/or thick. Soaking a tangled coat with water will only tighten the tangles, making them difficult, if not impossible, to remove. It is tempting to wash a dirty Poodle first, then brush. Don't. It just creates a bigger brushing job.

Brushing the Poodle correctly can be tricky, because there is usually so much to brush. It is important to brush down to the skin, without actually brushing the skin. This can be accomplished by pushing back, or parting, the coat with one hand and brushing the hair down a little at a time with the other. Use quick, deep strokes of the brush, and brush small areas. Do not rake the brush over the dog's skin. This will cause a condition known as brush-burn, in which the skin becomes red, irritated and uncomfortable. Pink- and light-skinned Poodles seem to be more sensitive to this.

Should the Poodle stand, sit or lie down while being brushed? That is really a personal preference. Choose whichever is easiest. Some people prefer that the dog stands; others find it easier when the dog lies down.

What about combing the Poodle? What type of comb is best? There are many styles of combs from which to choose, but the most durable and easy-to-clean combs are metal, either with or without a handle. For every-day purposes, a medium tooth-width is best. A fine-tooth "flea" comb should be used only for combing out fleas.

Combing should follow brushing. Once the Poodle is brushed thoroughly, run a comb through his locks to detect snarls missed by brushing. The comb is the perfect tool for finishing touches, such as smoothing or fluffing the coat.

CLIPPING NAILS

While the dog is standing, look to see if the nails touch the table. If they do, they probably need trimming. The idea is to keep the nails trimmed so they do not touch the ground—and you do not hear that telltale click-click down the hallway.

There are several types of nail trimmers on the market, and the one you select will depend upon your Poodle's size. Small or medium-size clippers work well for the Toy and Miniature; large, heavy-duty clippers are best suited for the Standard.

It is a good idea to purchase styptic powder. Sometimes it is difficult to avoid "quicking" a nail—that is, cutting it too short and making it bleed—so it is important to have this powder on hand to stop bleeding. To smooth the nails after clipping, purchase a file. A large metal file works well for this task.

To trim the nails, hold a paw firmly in one hand. Place your thumb on top of the foot and fingers underneath to spread the toes. With the clippers in your other hand, clip the nails, one at a time, with short, decisive strokes. Do not forget the dewclaws, which appear at wrist level.

At first, you may want to trim only the nail tips to avoid cutting down to the quick. Many professional groomers decide how much to trim by noticing where the nail starts to curl, then cutting at that point.

If you cut the nail too short (or if the quick has grown out too long) the Poodle will probably yelp, but try not to panic. Simply drop the clippers—keeping hold of the paw—and grab a pinch of styptic powder between your thumb and forefinger. Apply this to the bleeding nail and press. Hold it for thirty seconds or so. Continue until the bleeding stops.

File the nails on the first paw before moving on to the next paw. A few swipes of the file will usually remove any rough edges. If you did not cut the nails short enough with the clippers, use the file to take off more length. This takes more time, and often the dog resists this more than clipping.

Dogs probably detest nail clipping more than any other procedure, so do not be surprised if your Poodle fusses. To minimize difficulties, begin trimming the nails during puppyhood and be sure to praise the dog lavishly when he sits still for the procedure.

Eyes and Ears

Is there a bright sparkle in your Poodle's eyes? If so, they are probably healthy, and all you need to do is gently wipe the corners with a water-moistioned cotton ball. It is not a good idea to use eyedrops or other eye ointments unless they are prescribed by a veterinarian.

If you notice redness, cloudiness, excessive tearing or inflammation, call your veterinarian right away.

Ear care is more involved. Look inside the Poodle's ears. Healthy ears are clean, free of debris and without odor. Chances are there is hair growing in the Poodle's ear canal. This is normal for this breed, but it should be removed to help prevent infection and to make the ears easier to clean. (Opinions do vary as to whether or not the ear hair should be removed. Ask your vet what is best for your Poodle.)

Ear powder, a chalky white substance that makes the ear hair easier to grab and pull, can be purchased at pet-supply stores. To remove the hair, which should be done before cleaning, apply a small amount of powder into the ear canal and make sure the ear hair is covered with powder. While holding the ear flap back with one hand, gently pluck the hair with the thumb and forefinger of your other hand. Be sure to pull only the hair that grows in the ear canal. This does not hurt the Poodle, and most do not object to it. You may find, though, that if you pull hair that grows on the inside of the ear flap the dog will object.

Keeping the nails proper length is essential.

Generally, the Poodle's healthy ears will not need a lot of cleaning. Wipe them out with a dry cotton ball or one *slightly* moistened with mineral oil each time you groom (after pulling ear hair). There are many commercially prepared ear cleaners, though it may not be necessary to use one if the ears are clean. These products can contain alcohol, which some vets say irritates the ear lining. Ask your vet which cleaner, if any, is best for your Poodle.

Cleaning a dirty ear, one that is filled with wax or a dark brown waxy debris (a sign of ear mites), is another story. Dampen a cotton ball with mineral oil or ear cleaner and get to work. Hold the ear flap up with one hand and wipe with the other. Wrap the cotton ball around your finger and insert it as far into the canal as possible. Wipe out all folds and crevices, but do so gently. It may take several cotton balls to clean the ears thoroughly.

If the ear is extremely dirty or filled with dry, caked debris, you may want to fill the canal with ear cleaner

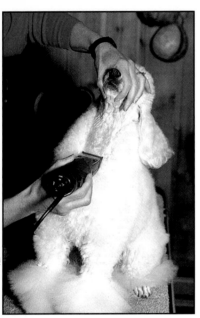

(per directions) before wiping it out with cotton balls. To do this, hold up the ear flap and squirt a small amount into the canal. Massage the base of the ear for a few minutes, then clean with a cotton ball.

You may notice that while cleaning her ears, your Poodle will have an overwhelming urge to shake. Take a time-out and let the dog shake, but take a few steps away from the grooming table before you do this. Otherwise, there is a good chance ear cleaner, mineral oil and whatever has loosened will end up all over you.

With consistency in place and procedure and a little bit of patience, grooming can be a positive experience for your Poodle.

Some dogs suffer from chronic ear problems, including bacterial infections, yeast or fungus infections, ear mites or ear allergies. Do not try to treat a sore, inflamed ear. Call your vet instead. The goal of ear care as part of the grooming routine is to prevent, not diagnose and treat.

HEALTHY TEETH

Examine your Poodle's teeth and gums for signs of disease. Are the gums inflamed? Are the teeth marred with tartar buildup? Does the dog's breath smell bad? Call the vet with questions regarding any of these suspicious symptoms.

Should you brush your Poodle's teeth? Absolutely! By beginning during puppyhood, the Poodle will accept the procedure quite well. Purchase a "doggie" toothbrush and toothpaste at a pet-supply store, then brush approximately once a week.

Some dogs will not tolerate having their teeth brushed. If yours is like this, try using a soft cloth wrapped around your index finger, or a ready-made dental pad from a pet-supply retailer. Wipe the teeth gently to remove food particles. Praise your dog for cooperating. Do not be tempted to scrape tartar off the dog's teeth; you may do more harm than good. Leave this job to a veterinarian who is trained in canine dental care.

And never use human toothpaste to brush your Poodle's teeth. It can cause severe digestive upset. Use only toothpaste formulated for dogs.

The Bath

It may seem odd that bathing is last on the grooming list, but it is for good reason. The coat must be brushed first or bathing will tighten the tangles, and styptic and ear powders are messy. Bathing enables you to cleanse a matt-free coat and remove powders.

The key to successful bathing is preparation. Before moving the dog from the grooming table to the tub, make sure you have shampoo, diluted flea dip if necessary, towels and cotton balls within reach. If the tub does not have a spray attachment, purchase one. It makes bathing much easier.

You also need a way to secure the Poodle in the tub to avoid having a wet, soapy dog running through the house. Groomers use a grooming noose; purchase one or use a non-leather collar and leash.

Once your dog is secured in the tub, place a cotton ball in each ear to keep water out. Saturate the dog with warm water, beginning at the top of the head. Work back, soaking the top of the head and the ears (do not spray directly in the dog's face or ears) and moving along the back to the tail. Begin at the head again, this time underneath the chin, to the neck, chest and front legs. Then soak the sides, stomach, rear end and, finally, the back legs. Be sure the dog is wet to the skin. It may take several moments of soaking to get through the Poodle's dense coat. Remember, this breed was originally bred to work in water and has the coat to prove it!

Apply shampoo, beginning with the head and working down the back to the tail. Take care not to get soap in the dog's eyes. Many groomers dilute shampoo in a plastic bucket and apply it with a sponge. Try it—it is easier than pouring shampoo from a bottle, saves on shampoo and ensures that the dog is soapy all over.

Once the dog is soapy, start scrubbing, literally. Massage the soap into the fur with your hands. Use the sponge to clean the stomach and genital areas. Rinse well, again beginning with the head and working down the back to the tail, then repeat the process.

The final rinse is especially important because soap left in the dog's coat will irritate his skin and look like flakes of dandruff. Once you think you have rinsed all the soap out, rinse again.

If you wish to apply flea dip, do so after the final rinse and leave on for a residual effect. A sponge is a handy tool for applying flea dip, too. Be sure to follow the manufacturer's directions for applying dip and do not use dip after using a flea shampoo. Such chemical combinations can be toxic.

Towel dry the dog while he is secured in the tub. It may take several towels to absorb the excess water, so be sure to have them handy before bathing.

FLUFF DRYING

Fluff drying is, for the most part, the secret to giving the Poodle a smooth, fluffed look. Because its coat is naturally curly, it will, when left to dry on its own, dry curly. Fluff drying—drying while brushing continuously—straightens and fluffs the coat. A fluff-dried coat looks beautiful and is easier to scissor and shape.

Fluff drying is by no means an easy task. It's tricky to learn how to brush dry the coat a little bit at a time before the rest of the coat dries on its own—curly.

Those willing to give it a try first need a few supplies: a soft slicker brush and a blow dryer, preferably one on a stand to leave both arms free. As with brushing, drying must be done systematically. Groomers all have different ideas about where to begin, but here is one plan of action:

Step 1. Fluff dry the top knot and ears. Keep a towel wrapped around the Poodle's body while you are doing this so as to keep the body coat from curling.

Step 2. Fluff dry the neck, chest and front legs, one at a time. Keep the towel wrapped around the middle and hindquarters.

Step 3. Fluff dry the tail pom, rear and back legs, one at a time.

Advance preparation will make grooming go smoothly.

Step 4. Fluff the remaining body area and stomach.

These steps will vary according to your dog's coat length and trim style. The idea is to fluff each part of the coat before it dries on its own.

The technique for fluff drying can be tricky, as well. Aim the dryer at one area, the top knot for example. Brush quickly and softly until the hair is completely dry. Be careful not to brush too hard; that will irritate the dog's skin. Once the top knot is dry, aim the dryer at one of the ears and begin drying, a few strands at a time. Brush constantly. Continue on to the rest of the coat. If the coat dries before you can fluff it, dampen it with water.

A Word About Trims

Every Poodle, whether pet or show dog, must be trimmed. Who trims the dog and how it is trimmed varies considerably. Breeders and handlers usually groom their own show dogs, which are trimmed in the accepted styles for the ring (as noted in Chapter 1). Some pet owners groom their Poodles; many use the services of a professional groomer. Styles for pet Poodles mirror those in the show ring, with a variety as numerous as the colors in the rainbow. You must decide who will trim your Poodle and in what style.

If you are thinking of trimming your dog, you must be very determined—and skilled. Trimming and scissoring the Poodle is really an art. Just as any artist must master basic techniques, so must an owner master grooming basics before picking up clippers and a pair of scissors. In other words, if you cannot use a brush properly, how can you expect to use a pair of sharp scissors safely?

Before deciding to trim your Poodle, consider the following:

- the cost of equipment, including electric clippers, blades and scissors

- the danger of scissors in unskilled hands

- the challenge of trimming a wiggly puppy or dog

- the years of practice required to perfect trimming skills

Styles for your pet Poodle are really a matter of personal preference. Some owners like simple utility trims; others like elaborate patterns. To get an idea of the many trims available, read grooming books (there are many good ones dedicated to grooming the Poodle), visit grooming shops or talk with other Poodle owners.

SELECTING A GROOMER

Fortunately, there are many skilled and kind professional groomers. But how do you choose one?

Ask your breeder, veterinarian or a fellow Poodle owner for a recommendation. Look through the Yellow Pages; pick several to call and visit (without the dog).

Meet with the groomer. Take note of her professionalism. Is she certified? (There are many excellent groomers who are not certified, but the industry is leaning toward mandatory certification.) Does she seem to genuinely love animals? Is she familiar with a variety of Poodle trims? Is she easy to communicate with? Is the shop clean? Is the pricing fair? Pay attention to first impressions.

After visiting a few shops, pick one. Next, make an appointment. Be sure to communicate clearly how you want the dog trimmed. If you're not sure, ask the groomer for ideas or suggestions.

Simple utility trims are easier for the pet owner to master.

A groomer is definitely one of your Poodle's best friends. Select one carefully.

chapter 7

Keeping your
Poodle
Healthy

You can help your dog maintain good health by practicing the art of preventive care. Preventive health care can be summed up in the adage, "An apple a day keeps the doctor away." In other words, take good care of your Poodle today and it will be healthy tomorrow.

The Importance of Preventive Care

There are many aspects of preventive care with which Poodle owners should be familiar: vaccinations, regular vet visits and tooth care are just some. The advantage of preventive care is that it *prevents* problems. Of course, health difficulties may still arise, but owners who are well versed in preventive care will minimize the severity of the problem, if one comes about.

The earlier that illness is detected in the Poodle, the easier it is for the veterinarian to treat the problem. Owners can help ensure the dog's health by being on the lookout for medical problems. All this requires is an eye for detail and a willingness to observe. Pay close attention to your Poodle, how he looks, how he acts. What is normal behavior? How does his coat usually look? What are his eating and sleeping patterns? Subtle changes can indicate a problem. Keep close tabs on what is normal for your Poodle, and if anything out of the ordinary develops call the veterinarian.

SPAYING AND NEUTERING

Spaying or neutering—surgically altering the Poodle so she or he cannot reproduce—should be at the top of every owner's "To Do" list. Why?

First, every day thousands of puppies are born in the United States as a result of uncontrolled breeding. For every pet living in a happy home today, there are four pets on the street or in abusive homes suffering from starvation, exposure, neglect or mistreatment. In six years, a single female dog and her offspring can be the source of 67,000 new dogs.

Finding homes for all the puppies born annually is a staggering task. It is further complicated by the responsibility of determining which homes are indeed caring ones. Will a new owner offer the pet all the love, patience and care the puppy deserves, or will he or she dispose of the animal as soon as it is no longer cuddly or convenient to care for? Even if a well-meaning owner is able to provide a good home for a pet, there are thousands of other animals that will never find homes.

A second reason to spay or neuter your Poodle is to create a healthier, more well-adjusted pet that, in most cases, will live longer than an intact animal. A spayed female is less prone to uterine, ovarian and mammary cancer, and the procedure eliminates the behavior that accompanies the female's heat cycle. A neutered male is less likely to develop prostate or anal cancer and is less apt to roam. Spraying and marking behavior are also reduced by altering.

Not only does spaying and neutering make the Poodle a better pet, it also reduces the number of animals taken in and euthanized at shelters each year.

When should your Poodle be spayed or neutered? Recommendations vary among vets, but six months

of age is commonly suggested. Ask your vet what age is best for your Poodle. Altering puppies as young as eight weeks has been the subject of great study in recent years. Early altering is practiced by many animal shelters wishing to eliminate any possibility of adopted pets producing more offspring.

Be kind to your Poodle: have it spayed or neutered.

VACCINATIONS

Another priority on a Poodle owner's list of preventive care is vaccinations. Vaccinations protect the dog against a host of infectious diseases, preventing an illness itself and the misery that accompanies it.

Vaccines work by creating immunity. The dog is exposed, usually via injection, to the organism that causes the disease. The organism has been artificially altered so that it elicits an immune response from the dog without causing the disease itself.

Vaccines should be a part of every young puppy's health care, since youngsters are so susceptible to disease. Most vaccines are given in a series while the dog is young, and yearly boosters are given thereafter. To remain effective, vaccinations must be kept current.

GOOD NUTRITION

Dogs that receive the appropriate nutrients daily will be healthier and stronger than those that do not. The proper balance of proteins, fats, carbohydrates, vitamins, minerals and sufficient water enables the dog to remain healthy by fighting off illness.

ROUTINE CHECKUPS

Regular visits to the veterinary clinic should begin when your Poodle is a young pup and continue throughout her life. Make this a habit and it will certainly contribute to your Poodle's good health. Even if your Poodle seems perfectly healthy, a checkup once or twice a year is in order. Even if your dog seems fine to you, she could have an ongoing problem. Your veterinarian is trained to notice subtle changes or hints of illness.

WELL-BEING

Aside from the dog's physical needs—a proper and safe shelter, nutritious diet, health care and regular exercise—the Poodle needs plenty of plain, old-fashioned love. True, dogs do not understand love in the same way people do. But accepting the dog into your family and caring for it is, in the dog's understanding, a sign that it has become a member of the "pack." Remember, all dogs are pack animals, with an innate understanding of a special canine social hierarchy, and they need each other, or people, to develop properly. The dog is happiest when it is part of a family, enjoying the social

---

ADVANTAGES OF SPAY/NEUTER

The greatest advantage of spaying (for females) or neutering (for males) your dog is that you are guaranteed your dog will not produce puppies. There are too many puppies already available for too few homes. There are other advantages as well.

ADVANTAGES OF SPAYING

No messy heats.

No "suitors" howling at your windows or waiting in your yard.

Decreased incidences of pyometra (disease of the uterus) and breast cancer.

ADVANTAGES OF NEUTERING

Lessens male aggressive and territorial behaviors, but doesn't affect the dog's personality. Behaviors are often owner-induced, so neutering is not the only answer, though it is a good start.

Prevents the need to roam in search of bitches in season.

Decreased incidences of urogenital diseases.

interactions, nurturing and play. Bringing the Poodle into the family "pack" provides the dog with a sense of security.

The Poodle needs mental stimulation as well, especially because the breed is so intelligent. Obedience training is an excellent way to encourage your dog to use her mind. Remember, Poodles will use their brilliant minds in some manner, so it is best to direct them in a positive way.

SIGNS OF ILLNESS

Spotting illness in your Poodle early will go a long way toward a positive and safe prognosis. Actually recognizing specific signs of illness can be difficult, though. Owners must be sensitive to subtle, and sometimes not-so-subtle, signs that can indicate disease. Take note of the following list and be on the lookout for any of these:

- Changes in behavior. A normally outgoing dog may appear depressed and withdrawn.

- Changes in appetite, water intake, urination or bowel movements.

- Apparent pain or sensitivity to touch.

- Dull hair coat or excessive hair loss.

- Weight loss.

- Vomiting or diarrhea.

- Blood in urine.

- Fever or runny nose and eyes.

- Swelling or lumps.

- Lethargy.

- Convulsions or choking.

- Unusual odor.

- Strained or shallow breathing.

Common Diseases

Unfortunately, even with the best preventive care, the Poodle can fall ill. Infectious diseases, which are commonly spread from dog to dog via infected urine, feces or other body secretions, can wreak havoc. Following are a few of the diseases that can affect your Poodle.

RABIES

Probably one of the most well-known diseases that can affect dogs, rabies can strike any warm-blooded animal—and is fatal. The rabies virus, which is present in an affected animal's saliva, is usually spread through a bite or open wound. Fortunately, vaccination programs in the United States for domestic animals have prevented this fatal disease from spreading. Its incidence is rare among domestic animals and people, and it is found sporadically in wild animals such as skunks, bats, raccoons or foxes. The rabies incidence in countries without similar rigid vaccination standards is much higher.

> ### YOUR PUPPY'S VACCINES
>
> Vaccines are given to prevent your dog from getting an infectious disease like canine distemper or rabies. Vaccines are the ultimate preventive medicine: they're given before your dog ever gets the disease so as to protect him from the disease. That's why it is necessary for your dog to be vaccinated routinely. Puppy vaccines start at eight weeks of age for the five-in-one DHLPP vaccine and are given every three to four weeks until the puppy is sixteen months old. Your veterinarian will put your puppy on a proper schedule and will remind you when to bring in your dog for shots.

There are two types of rabies: furious and paralytic. Their average incubation period in dogs is three to eight weeks, but it can be as short as a week or as long as one year.

The signs of the disease can be subtle at first. Normally friendly pets can become irritable and withdrawn. Shy pets may become overly friendly. Eventually, the dog becomes withdrawn and avoids light, which hurts the eyes of a rabid dog. Fever, vomiting and diarrhea are common.

Once these symptoms develop, the animal will die; there is no treatment or cure.

Since rabid animals may have a tendency to be aggressive and bite, animals suspected of having rabies should only be handled by animal control handlers or veterinarians.

Rabies is preventable with routine vaccines, and such vaccinations are required by law for domestic animals in many states in this country.

PARVOVIRUS

Canine parvovirus is a highly contagious and devastating illness. The hardy virus is usually transmitted through contaminated feces, but it can be carried on an infected dog's feet or skin. It strikes dogs of all ages and is most serious in young puppies.

There are two main types of parvovirus. The first signs of the diarrhea-syndrome type are usually depression and lack of appetite, followed by vomiting and the characteristic bloody diarrhea. The dog appears to be in great pain, and he usually has a high fever.

The cardiac-syndrome type affects the heart muscle and is most common in young puppies. Puppies with this condition will stop nursing, whine and gasp for air. Death may occur suddenly or in a few days. Youngsters that recover can have lingering heart failure that eventually takes their life.

Veterinarians can treat dogs with parvovirus, but the outcome varies. It depends on the age of the animal and severity of the disease. Treatment may include fluid therapy, medication to stop the severe diarrhea and antibiotics to prevent or stop secondary infection.

Young puppies receive some antibody protection against the disease from their mother, but they lose it quickly and must be vaccinated to prevent the disease. In most cases, vaccinated puppies are protected against the disease.

CORONAVIRUS

Canine coronavirus is especially devastating to young puppies, causing depression, lack of appetite, vomiting that may contain blood and characteristically yellow-orange diarrhea. The virus is transmitted through feces, urine and saliva, and the onset of symptoms is usually rapid.

Dogs suffering from coronavirus are treated similarly to those suffering from parvovirus: fluid therapy, medication to stop diarrhea and vomiting and antibiotics if necessary.

Vaccinations are available to protect puppies and dogs against the virus and are recommended especially for those dogs in frequent contact with other dogs.

DISTEMPER

Caused by a virus, the highly contagious distemper is the leading cause of infectious disease in dogs.

A healthy Poodle fares well in the show ring.

The virus is similar to the virus that causes measles in humans. It is most common in unvaccinated puppies aged three to eight months, but older dogs are susceptible as well.

The distemper virus is hardy and can live for many years. Incidence of distemper appears higher in the spring because the virus lies dormant in the earth, which is frozen during winter. Warm temperatures bring the spring thaw and reactivate the virus.

The distemper virus frequently attacks the epithelial cells, which are found on the skin, eye membranes, breathing tubes and mucus membranes of the intestines. How a dog responds to distemper varies: Some are extremely ill and others are not. It often depends upon the dog's condition prior to illness.

Distemper takes a variety of forms, and secondary infections and complications are common. Treatment is complex, and success varies. The sooner the dog is treated, the better the prognosis.

71

Current vaccinations will prevent distemper in dogs, and it is especially important to vaccinate bitches before breeding to ensure maternal antibodies in the pups.

HEPATITIS

Infectious canine hepatitis (*canine adenovirus-1*) can affect dogs of every age, but it is most severe in puppies. It primarily affects the dog's liver, kidneys and lining of the blood vessels. Highly contagious, it is transmitted through urine, feces and saliva. Infectious canine hepatitis is not to be confused with hepatitis that affects humans. The diseases are species-specific,

Check your dog's teeth frequently and brush them regularly.

meaning that infectious canine hepatitis can only be transmitted dog to dog.

This disease has several forms. In the fatal fulminating form, the dog becomes ill very suddenly, develops bloody diarrhea and dies. In the acute form, the dog develops a fever, has bloody diarrhea, vomits blood and refuses to eat. Jaundice may be present; the whites of the dog's eyes appear yellow. Dogs with a mild case are lethargic or depressed and often refuse to eat.

Infectious canine hepatitis must be diagnosed and confirmed with a blood test. Ill dogs require hospitalization.

Hepatitis is preventable in dogs by keeping vaccinations current.

LYME DISEASE

Lyme disease has received a lot of press recently, with its increased incidence throughout the United States. The illness, caused by the bacteria *Borrelia burgdorferi*, is carried by ticks. It is passed along when the tick bites a victim, canine or human. (The dog cannot pass the disease to people, though. It is only transmitted via the tick.) It is most common during the tick season in May through August.

In dogs, the disease manifests itself in sudden lameness, caused by swollen joints, similar to arthritis. The dog is weak and may run a fever. The lameness can last a few days or several months, and some dogs have recurring difficulties.

Antibiotics are very effective in treating Lyme disease, and the sooner it is diagnosed and treated, the better. A vaccine is available; ask your veterinarian if your dog would benefit from it.

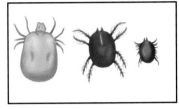

Three types of ticks (l-r): the wood tick, brown dog tick and deer tick.

TETANUS

Tetanus, or "lockjaw," can affect dogs, other animals and people. It is not contagious. Dogs are naturally resistant to this disease, though vaccinations are recommended for some working dogs.

The bacteria that causes the disease, *Clostridium tetani*, is commonly found in soil contaminated by cow or horse manure. Tetanus is spread by infecting an open cut or puncture wound.

Signs of tetanus can appear a few days after injury or can be delayed for weeks. They include spasms and rigid extension of the legs, difficulty opening the mouth and swallowing (hence the term "lockjaw") and retraction of the lips and eyeballs. Prompt treatment is required to prevent the dog from dying.

LEPTOSPIROSIS

Canine leptospirosis is caused by the spirochete bacteria, and it is transmitted through the urine of infected animals. Rats are believed to be the main carriers of the disease.

Signs of illness appear five to fifteen days after the dog ingests or comes in contact with infected urine. Fever is common, as is loss of appetite, depression and listlessness. The disease usually attacks the kidneys, and the dog may appear to have great pain in the kidney area. Vomiting and diarrhea may be present.

Blood or urine tests are used to determine the pre sence of the bacteria. Hospitalization is required, and dogs are treated with fluid therapy, antibiotics and medication to control vomiting and diarrhea. Special cautions must be taken with dogs infected with le tospirosis, as the bacteria can be shed in the urine for up to a year following illness. To avoid infecting other an mals, urine and feces must be tho ough- ly cleaned up.

In areas where leptospirosis is a problem, vaccinations are recom- mended.

Use tweezers to remove ticks from your dog.

INFECTIOUS TRACHEOBRONCHITIS

Commonly called "kennel cough," or the more politically correct "canine cough," this con- tagious disease shows itself as a harsh, dry cough. It has been termed "kennel cough," much to the dismay of kennel owners, because of its often rapid spread through kennels. The cough may persist for weeks and is often followed by a bout of chronic bronchitis.

A number of viruses have been tagged as causing this persistent problem, including the adenovirus types 1 and 2, herpes virus in the adult and parai fluenza. Immunizing the dog with the hepatitis vaccine protects against adenovirus. The parainfluenza vaccine protects against canine parainfluenza virus.

Many kennels require proof of vaccination against certain viruses before boarding. If your dog is in and out of kennels frequently, vaccination certainly is not a bad idea.

Bordetella is frequently found in dogs recovering from a viral respiratory problem. The bacteria, *B. Bronchiseptica*, attacks the dog's weakened immune system causing further respiratory illness. The bacteria has also been isolated in dogs suffering from the "kennel cough" syndrome.

Two vaccines, intranasal and injection, are available to prevent bordetella. Puppies as young as two to four weeks can be protected with the intranasal form; normally the injection is given at 8 to 12 weeks.

BRUCELLOSIS

Caused by the bacteria *Brucella canis*, brucellosis causes reproductive failure in dogs. It is the leading cause of late miscarriages, and it may be attributed to stillborn puppies or puppies that die shortly after birth. It can cause sterility in both the male and female dog.

Signs of an active infection include swollen and painful lymph nodes and joints. The testicles in the male may swell, then atrophy. The disease is transmittable between mating dogs, and it may be transmitted to puppies through the mother's milk.

A test for the disease is recommended before mating. Presently, there is no vaccine or treatment or cure for brucellosis.

> ### WHEN TO CALL THE VET
>
> In any emergency situation, you should call your veterinarian immediately. You can make the difference in your dog's life by staying as calm as possible when you call and by giving the doctor or the assistant as much information as possible before you leave for the clinic. That way, the vet will be able to take immediate, specific action to remedy your dog's situation.
>
> Emergencies include acute abdominal pain, suspected poisoning, snakebite, burns, frostbite, shock, dehydration, abnormal vomiting or bleeding, and deep wounds. You are the best judge of your dog's health, as you live with and observe him every day. Don't hesitate to call your veterinarian if you suspect trouble.

Emergency Situations

WHAT IS NORMAL?

It's 11 P.M. and your Poodle is sick. You're not sure if you should call the veterinarian right away or wait until morning. How can you determine if your Poodle needs immediate attention or care within twenty-four hours? What constitutes an emergency situation?

To make such a determination, it is important to be familiar with the dog's normal vital signs: temperature,

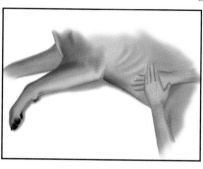

pulse and respiration rate. To know what is abnormal, owners must know what is normal.

Look at your Poodle's gums. Are they healthy and pink? Now press the gums with a finger; the gum color will pale as it is pressed. See how quickly it returns to normal. This is called *capillary refill time*. It should take a second or two, but it will take longer if the animal is in shock.

Applying abdominal thrusts can save a choking dog.

Look at your Poodle from head to tail. Notice his eyes (are they normally bright?); his skin—when gently pulled it should immediately fall back into place (severe dehydration prohibits this); and the rest of his body (is the Poodle normally sensitive anywhere?). Know your Poodle's normal physical state so you can have a point of reference for comparison.

If your Poodle becomes ill or suffers a trauma, keep a cool head and evaluate her physical condition. Then determine if an immediate call to the vet is in order. *If there is ever any doubt of how serious the injury is, do not hesitate to call.*

Normally, a Poodle's vital signs are:

> Temperature: 100–102.5 degrees F.
>
> Pulse: 60–169 per minute for adult dogs; up to 180 in Toy breeds; 220 for puppies.
>
> Respirations: 10–30 per minute at rest.

First Aid

First aid is not a substitute for professional care, though it can help save a dog's life.

To Stop Bleeding

Bleeding from a severe cut or wound must be stopped right away. There are two basic techniques—direct pressure and the tourniquet.

Try to control bleeding first by using direct pressure. Ask an assistant to hold the injured Poodle and place several pads of sterile gauze over the wound. Press. Do not wipe the wound or apply any cleansers or ointments. Apply firm, even pressure. If blood soaks through the pad, do not remove it as this could disrupt clotting. Simply place another pad on top and continue to apply pressure.

If bleeding on a leg or the tail does not stop by applying pressure, try using a tourniquet. Use this only as a last resort. A tourniquet that is left on too long can result in limb loss. To apply a tourniquet, do the following:

1. Wrap the limb or tail with one-inch gauze or a wide piece of cloth slightly above the wound and tie a half knot. Do not use a narrow band, rope or wire.

2. Place a pencil or stick on top and finish the knot.

3. Twist the pencil slowly until the bleeding stops. Fasten in place with tape.

4. Cover the wound with sterile gauze.

5. Once the tourniquet is on, take the dog to your veterinarian right away.

If the dog is bleeding from her mouth or anus, or vomits or defecates blood, she may be suffering from internal injuries. Do not attempt to stop bleeding. Call the veterinarian right away for emergency treatment.

CPR

Cardiopulmonary resuscitation, commonly called CPR, is a life-saving technique that provides artificial breathing and heart contractions for an unconscious animal whose heart and breathing have stopped. CPR combines artificial breathing with heart massage. Artificial respiration alone can be used for animals suffering respiratory distress—not combined with cardiac arrest—to aid breathing.

Dogs can suffer respiratory and cardiac failure for many reasons, including being hit by a car, poisoning or electrical shock. Respiratory distress is caused by many conditions, including a foreign object in the nasal passages, chest wounds or tearing of the diaphragm.

Do not attempt to perform CPR on a dog that has a heartbeat, or perform artificial respiration on a conscious dog, unless his breathing is extremely shallow. In these instances, the life-saving techniques can harm an animal.

 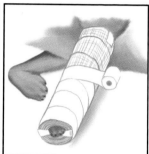

Make a temporary splint by wrapping the leg in firm casing, then bandaging it.

Artificial respiration: There are two methods of artificial respiration: *chest compression* and *mouth-to-nose*. Chest compression works by applying force to the chest wall, which pushes air out and allows the natural recoil of the chest to draw air in. Mouth-to-nose is forced respiration. It is used when the compression technique fails or when the chest is punctured.

To perform artificial respiration/chest compression:

1. Lay the animal on his right side and remove collar and harness.

2. Open the animal's mouth and check for possible obstructions.

3. Place both hands on the chest and press down sharply. Release quickly. If done properly, air should move in and out. If not, perform mouth-to-nose respiration.

4. Continue until the dog breathes on his own or as long as the heart beats.

To perform artificial respiration/mouth-to-nose:

1. Perform number 1 and 2 from above.
2. Pull the tongue forward and close the mouth.
3. Place your mouth over your dog's nose and blow in steadily for three seconds. The chest will expand. Release for exhale.
4. Continue until the dog breathes on his own or as long as the heart beats.

Heart massage: Heart massage is used when there is no pulse, which often follows a cessation of breathing. To perform:

1. Feel for pulse or heartbeat.
2. Open the animal's mouth and check for possible obstructions.
3. Lay the animal on her right side and remove collar and harness.
4. Place your thumb on one side of the sternum and fingers on the other side just below the elbows. For large dogs, place the heel of your hand on the rib cage behind the elbow, which is directly over the heart.
5. With hands in this position, squeeze firmly to compress the chest. Do so five to six times. Wait five seconds to let the chest expand and repeat.

A FIRST-AID KIT

Keep a canine first-aid kit on hand for general care and emergencies. Check it periodically to make sure liquids haven't spilled or dried up, and replace medications and materials after they're used. Your kit should include:

Activated charcoal tablets

Adhesive tape
(1 and 2 inches wide)

Antibacterial ointment
(for skin and eyes)

Aspirin (buffered or enteric coated, *not* Ibuprofen)

Bandages: Gauze rolls (1 and 2 inches wide) and dressing pads

Cotton balls

Diarrhea medicine

Dosing syringe

Hydrogen peroxide (3%)

Petroleum jelly

Rectal thermometer

Rubber gloves

Rubbing alcohol

Scissors

Tourniquet

Towel

Tweezers

6. Continue until the heart beats on its own or until no pulse is felt for five minutes.

Combining heart massage and artificial respiration may require two people, one to massage and one to respirate. In an emergency situation where no help is available, after five cardiac massages perform one artificial (mouth-to-nose) respiration without breaking the rhythm of the massages.

SHOCK

Trauma, such as being hit by a car, blood loss, burns or allergic reactions, can cause a condition known as shock. Shock is a collapse of the circulatory system. It occurs when the volume of circulating blood is decreased or the blood vessels collapse, and the heart loses its ability to pump blood. This decreased supply of oxygen to the tissues usually results in unconsciousness, pale gums, weak, rapid pulse and labored, rapid breathing.

Shock can be difficult to recognize, but it must be treated right away because it can be fatal. If the dog is in shock:

1. Stop bleeding or give CPR as necessary.
2. Allow the dog to adopt a position in which she is most comfortable.
3. Cover the dog with a towel or blanket.
4. If the dog is unconscious, clear her airways and slightly elevate her rear end. This will assist in blood flow to the brain.
5. Do not give the dog water. Due to decreased blood circulation, the digestive tract cannot absorb the water efficiently.
6. Do not muzzle the dog. This may impair breathing.
7. Transport the dog to the veterinary clinic on a stretcher, flat board or hammock for treatment right away.

Handling an Injured Dog

An injured Poodle is a dog in pain, which means he will quite frequently respond to those trying to help by growling, snapping or biting. Owners must be aware of this tendency and be prepared before handling or moving an injured animal.

Approach the injured dog carefully and from behind, if possible. Speak softly and move slowly. Try to reassure the dog, possibly by petting him. Do not excite or stress the animal.

The dog may need to be muzzled before handling or transporting him to the veterinary clinic. Do so gently and calmly (see pages 90–91 on "Muzzling").

If the dog is small, he may be carried by hand; larger dogs should be placed on a stretcher or flat board and carried.

Pick up an injured dog very carefully. The idea is to avoid further injury. Gently slide one hand underneath the animal's rear end and your other hand under the chest (for large dogs, use two people). Make sure the dog's weight is distributed evenly to avoid twisting or bending the body. Slowly slide the animal onto a blanket or towel or, preferably, a stretcher. Cover the animal with a towel or blanket and speak soothingly to him.

Run your hands regularly over your dog to feel for any injuries.

Poisoning

The curious nature of the dog often leads her to eat or lick items she shouldn't. Unfortunately, many substances are poisonous to dogs, including household products, plants or chemicals. Owners must learn to act quickly if poisoning is suspected because the results can be deadly.

If your dog appears to be poisoned:

- Call your veterinarian and follow his or her directions.

- Try to identify the poison source—this is really important. Take the container or plant to the clinic.

- Induce vomiting if you are sure the dog has ingested a poisonous substance, and if you are sure the substance is *not* kerosene, turpentine, drain cleaner, tranquilizers or sharp objects, or that more than two hours has passed since the poison was swallowed.

- Do not try to induce vomiting in a semi- or unconscious animal.

- Transport the dog to the clinic as directed by the vet. Bring with you the telephone number for the National Animal Poison Control Center (listed below).

Some of the many house-hold substances harmful to your dog.

Once the dog arrives at the clinic, your veterinarian may induce vomiting, if you have not done so already, and give him activated charcoal to delay absorption of the poison. Specific antidotes will be given depending upon the type of poison.

If your Poodle has not ingested a poison but has it on his skin or coat, bathe him in warm water with a mild shampoo. Prevent the dog from licking prior to the bath to prevent ingestion.

There are many poison control centers throughout the United States, and it is a good idea to keep the telephone number of one near the telephone. The National Animal Poison Control Center hot line at the University of Illinois is one such organization, which is aimed specifically at pet poisonings. There are two numbers to call: an 800 number for emergencies, and a 900 number for non-emergency situations. The emergency 800 line can be used by veterinarians or pet owners for emergency poisoning information. Although it is an 800 number, callers are charged $30 per case. Callers to the 900 line must pay $20 for the first five minutes and $2.95 a minute thereafter, with a minimum charge of $20.

You can call the National Animal Poison Control Center hot line at (800) 548-2423 or (900) 680-0000, seven days a week.

HEATSTROKE

If it seems hot outside to an owner, it's a good bet the dog feels hot, too. Dogs do not tolerate high temperatures as well as people do, making them susceptible to heatstroke. To cool down, dogs pant to exchange air. When the air temperature is close to the dog's body temperature, difficulties can arise.

Heatstroke can be deadly and must be treated immediately to save the dog. Signs include rapid panting, darker-than-usual gums and tongue, salivating, exhaustion or vomiting. The dog's body temperature is elevated, sometimes as high as 106 degrees. If the dog is not treated, coma and death can follow.

If heatstroke is suspected, cool down your overheated dog as quickly as possible. Mildly affected dogs can be moved to a cooler environment, into an air-conditioned home, for example, or wrapped in moistened towels.

Take your dog's temperature (see pages 91–92 on "Taking a Temperature"). If it is over 104 degrees or if your dog seems unsteady, he must be cooled by immersion in a tub of cool water or hosed down with a garden hose. For a temperature over 106 or if your dog seems ready to collapse, a cool water enema is in order. The idea is to drop the dog's body temperature rapidly.

INSECT BITES/STINGS

Just like people, dogs can suffer bee stings and insect bites. Bees, wasps and yellow jackets leave a nasty, painful sting, and if your dog is stung repeatedly shock can occur.

If an insect bite is suspected, try to identify the culprit. Remove the stinger if it is a bee sting, and apply a mixture of baking soda and water to the sting. It is also a good idea to apply ice packs to reduce inflammation and ease pain. Call your veterinarian, especially if your dog seems ill or goes into shock.

Internal Parasites

Dogs are susceptible to several internal parasites, parasitic worms—roundworms, tapeworms, hookworms, whipworms and heartworms—that can cause great harm to the animal if left unchecked. Keeping your Poodle free of internal parasites is another important aspect of health care.

Most dogs suffer an invasion of one or more of these organisms at least once in their lives. Young and weak animals are especially susceptible. The signs of infestation are similar regardless of the type of parasite that has invaded the dog's body. Watch for general signs of poor condition: a dull haircoat, weight loss, lethargy, coughing, weakness and diarrhea.

For proper diagnosis and treatment of internal parasites, consult a veterinarian. Although the signs are similar, different types of parasites respond to different types and dosages of medication. A veterinarian can diagnose the exact type of parasite by examining your dog's stool, blood and urine samples, and will prescribe the appropriate treatment. Avoid over-the-counter deworming medications.

Dogs like to put things in their mouths making them more susceptible to internal parasites.

ROUNDWORMS

Roundworms, or ascarids, are probably the most common worms that affect dogs. Most puppies are born with these organisms in their intestines, which is why youngsters are treated for these parasites as soon as it is safe to do so.

Animals contract roundworms by ingesting soil and feces, or by ingesting chicken, rodent or other animal tissues that are contaminated with roundworm eggs. A roundworm infestation can rob vital nutrients from young puppies and cause diarrhea, vomiting and digestive upset. Roundworms can also harm a young animal's liver and lungs, so treatment is imperative.

TAPEWORMS

Tapeworms are commonly transmitted by fleas to dogs. Tapeworm eggs enter the body of a canine host when the animal accidentally ingests a carrier flea. The parasite settles in the intestines, where it sinks its head into the intestinal wall and feeds off material the host is digesting. The worm grows a body of egg packets, which break off periodically and are expelled from the body in the feces. Fleas then ingest the eggs from the feces and the parasite's life cycle begins all over again.

FIGHTING FLEAS

Remember, the fleas you see on your dog are only part of the problem—the smallest part! To rid your dog and home of fleas, you need to treat your dog *and* your home. Here's how:

- Identify where your pet(s) sleeps. These are "hot spots."

- Clean your pets' bedding regularly by vacuuming and washing.

- Spray "hot spots" with a nontoxic, long-lasting flea larvicide.

- Treat outdoor "hot spots" with insecticide.

- Kill eggs on pets with a product containing insect growth regulators (IGRs).

- Kill fleas on pets per your veterinarian's recommendation.

HOOKWORMS

Hookworms are so named because they hook onto an animal's small intestine and suck the host's blood. Like roundworms, hookworms are contracted when a dog ingests contaminated soil or feces.

The flea is a die-hard pest.

Hookworms can be especially devastating to dogs. They will become thin and sick; puppies can die. An affected dog will suffer from bloody diarrhea and, if the parasites migrate to the lungs, the dog may contract bronchitis or pneumonia.

Hookworms commonly strike puppies two to eight weeks of age and are less common in adult dogs.

WHIPWORMS

Known for their thread-like appearance, whipworms attach into the wall of the large intestine to feed. Thick-shelled eggs are passed in the feces and in about two to four weeks are mature and able to reinfect a host that ingests the eggs.

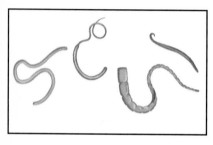

Mild whipworm infestation is often without signs, but as the worms grow, weight loss, bloody diarrhea and anemia follow. In areas where the soil is heavily contaminated, frequent checks are advised to prevent severe infestation.

Common internal parasites (l-r): roundworm, whipworm, tapeworm and hookworm.

HEARTWORMS

Heartworms are transmitted by the ordinary mosquito, but the effects are far from ordinary. Infection begins when the larvae from an infected mosquito are laid on the dog's skin. They burrow into the skin, or are ingested when the dog licks. In three to four months the larvae (microfilaria) become small worms and make their way to a vein, where they are transported to the heart. The worms burrow into the heart, grow and reproduce.

At first, a dog with heartworms is free of symptoms. The signs vary, but the most common is a deep cough and shortness of breath. The dog tires easily, is weak and loses weight. Eventually, the dog may suffer from congestive heart failure.

Treating heartworms is complex and difficult. The cure is often as devastating as the disease because the medications used to kill the worms and larvae are potentially toxic and dangerous; hospitalization is required. It is much easier to prevent a heartworm problem. Have your dog tested and put on a regular heartworm preventive—your veterinarian can advise you on exactly what to do.

External Parasites

Not only can internal parasites attack the Poodle, but a host of external pests—*fleas, ticks, lice* and *microscopic mites*—can strike, too.

Besides carrying tapeworm larvae, fleas bite and suck the host's blood. Their bites itch and are extremely annoying to dogs, especially if the dog is hypersensitive to the bite. Fleas must be eliminated on the dog with special shampoos and dips. Fleas also infest the dog's bedding and the owner's home and yard.

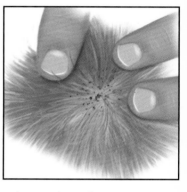

Several varieties of ticks attach themselves to dogs, where they burrow into the skin and suck blood. Ticks can be carriers of several diseases, including Lyme disease and Rocky Mountain Spotted Fever.

These specks in your dog's fur mean he has fleas.

Lice are not common in dogs, but when they are present they cause intense irritation and itching. There are two types: biting and sucking. Biting lice feed on skin scales, and sucking lice feed on blood.

There are several types of mites that cause several kinds of mange, including sarcoptic, demodectic and cheyletiella. These microscopic mites cause intense itching and misery to the dog.

Genetic Predispositions

Some health problems that affect Poodles are the result of breeding; they are inherited conditions passed down through family lines. Unfortunately, this is not uncommon in purebred dogs today. These problems are often the result of ignorance or poor

87

breeding practices, as little was known about inheritable diseases in early U.S. breeding programs. Many problems result from recessive genes, making them difficult to detect, and many conditions do not show up until the dog is older, perhaps after she has been bred.

HIP DYSPLASIA

Hip dysplasia, most common in Standard Poodles, is a condition in which the hips undergo progressive structural changes, eventually leading to lameness. The first signs of the problem are joint laxity, followed by abnormal gait, stiffness and lameness. It can be severely crippling. Primarily an inherited disease, even parents free of the condition can produce affected pups.

Diagnosis is made by taking X-rays and examining the hips for changes, including erosion of the joints, subluxation and arthritic changes.

The Orthopedic Foundation for Animals is dedicated to eradicating hip dysplasia from breeding lines. The organization, which consists of radiologists, reviews X-rays of dogs (for a fee). If the hips are normal for the particular breed, the dog is "certified" and assigned a number. Dogs must be twenty-four months old or older.

Responsible Poodle breeders, especially Standard breeders, screen for hip dysplasia. Those considering purchasing a Standard puppy should make sure the parents and grandparents are OFA certified. This is

---

IDENTIFYING YOUR DOG

It's a terrible thing to think about, but your dog could somehow, someday, get lost or stolen. How would you get him back? Your best bet would be to have some form of identification on your dog. You can choose from a collar and tags, a tattoo, a microchip or a combination of these three.

Every dog should wear a buckle collar with identification tags. They are the quickest and easiest way for a stranger to identify your dog. It's best to inscribe the tags with your name and phone number; you don't need to include your dog's name.

There are two ways to permanently identify your dog. The first is a tattoo, placed on the inside of your dog's thigh. The tattoo should be your social security number or your dog's AKC registration number.

The second is a microchip, a rice-sized pellet that's inserted under the dog's skin at the base of the neck, between the shoulder blades. When a scanner is passed over the dog, it will beep, notifying the person that the dog has a chip. The scanner will then show a code, identifying the dog. Microchips are becoming more and more popular and are certainly the wave of the future.

almost a guarantee that the dog will not develop hip dysplasia, but there is always the chance the problem may arise.

Progressive Retinal Atrophy

Progressive retinal atrophy (PRA), found in all sizes but most common in the smaller Poodles, is another inheritable disease. PRA causes the retina to degenerate gradually and eventually leads to blindness. It usually comes on late, when the dog is five to seven years old.

The Canine Eye Registration Foundation Inc. "certifies" dogs free of eye disease, including PRA, and collects research on canine eye disease. Again, reputable breeders routinely screen for PRA and certify their dogs free of the condition.

Congenital Epilepsy

Congenital epilepsy is another condition found in Poodles. Epilepsy is a recurrent seizure disorder, causing seizures, "fits" or convulsions. Affected dogs may jerk uncontrollably, foam at the mouth, collapse and lose normal consciousness. Seizures are caused by a burst of electrical activity in the brain.

While there is no cure for the condition, it can be controlled somewhat successfully with medication. Dogs with congenital epilepsy should not be bred, and before purchasing a Poodle you should research his family line carefully for the problem.

An Elizabethan collar keeps your dog from licking a fresh wound.

Miscellaneous

Anal Glands

Anal glands or anal sacs are positioned on either side of, and slightly below, the dog's anus. They contain a fluid secretion that normally is discharged into, then out through, the anus. At times, this secretion collects in the sacs, becoming thick, gummy and offensive in odor. The impacted fluid causes discomfort, and the dog may scoot on his rear to try to relieve the pressure.

A dog that scoots or licks its rear excessively may be suffering from impacted anal glands. Call your veterinarian so he or she can express the glands, which will make your dog more comfortable and prevent infection.

Many owners express the glands themselves, and some groomers do it for their customers, but this is not recommended because, if done improperly, it can do more harm than good. For the most part, the Poodle's anal glands require little attention; if they do, however, ask a vet for help.

Grooming is a good time to check your Poodle for external parasites.

MUZZLING

There are times when a dog must be muzzled to prevent him from biting. A injured dog, for example, is in pain and may snap and bite anyone who gets too close. To prevent the dog from hurting himself or others, muzzling him becomes necessary.

There is a simple way to do this safely, using a strip of cloth, necktie or stocking—any material that is strong but soft, several feet long and a few inches across.

Loop the material around the dog's muzzle and tie securely in a half knot on top of the muzzle. Then tie another half knot under the dog's chin. This will tie the dog's mouth shut.

Bring the ends of the material back, behind and just below the ears. Tie a full knot at the back of the dog's head.

It is important to note that some dogs react unfavorably to muzzling. An already excited dog may become more excited or stressed, especially since he is unable to pant while this type of muzzle is in place. Be sure to apply the muzzle slowly and calmly. Talk to your dog soothingly.

There are ready-made muzzles on the market that still prevent the dog from biting and work a little differently. These metal or leather muzzles fit over the muzzle, but do not keep the dog's mouth closed, and they buckle or snap behind the ears. Dogs seem to tolerate this type a little better. The disadvantage is that some dogs are able, with a little creative pawing, to pull off the muzzle.

Whatever type of muzzle you use, do not leave it on any longer than necessary.

TAKING A TEMPERATURE

To get the most accurate reading, your dog's temperature must be taken rectally. To do so:

1. Use a rectal thermometer. Shake down to 96 degrees F.

2. Lubricate the thermometer with petroleum jelly.

3. With the dog standing, raise her tail and gently insert the thermometer.

4. Do not allow the dog to sit; ask an assistant to help hold the dog if she fails to cooperate.

5. Do not let go of the thermometer. Hold it in place for three to four minutes.

6. Remove, wipe clean of fecal matter and read. The average temperature of an adult dog is 100 to 102.5 degrees F.

7. Clean the thermometer with alcohol before putting away to prevent the spread of disease.

Use a scarf or old hose to make a temporary muzzle, as shown.

Should the thermometer break when inserted, which is highly unlikely, do not attempt to retrieve the broken section. Call your veterinarian immediately.

TAKING A PULSE

To find out your dog's heartbeats per minute, place several fingers on the inside of the thigh where the leg joins the body. Press until the pulse is felt. The dog can be standing or lying down. Count the number of beats in fifteen seconds and multiply by four to get the per-minute rate. Alternatively, you can place several fingers on your dog's chest just behind the left elbow.

The average pulse is 60 to 160 beats per minute.

ADMINISTERING PILLS AND LIQUID MEDICINE

This can be tricky, since pills or liquid medicine do not always taste good—and Poodles know this. Giving medicine as directed by your vet is essential, though.

To give a pill, open the mouth wide then drop it in the back of the throat.

One method of giving a pill is simply to open your dog's mouth, place the pill at the very back of the throat, close the muzzle and hold it shut until the dog swallows. With any luck, the pill will go down. A little gentle stroking on the throat will help encourage your dog to swallow.

Another method is to wrap the pill in something tasty and simply feed it to your dog. Cheese, a tiny bit of meat or even peanut butter are common choices. Frequently, though, Poodles will ingest the tidbit and spit out the pill.

Sometimes crushing the pill and adding it to food or mixing it with water works. Note that some medicines are best given in their pill form, though. Check with your vet before taking this approach.

A good way to administer liquid medicine is to draw the correct dosage into a large, needleless syringe and squirt it into the mouth. To do this, gently hold your dog's mouth closed and place the syringe into the side of the mouth. Squirt a small amount at a time, allowing your dog to swallow before giving more.

EYE AND EAR MEDICATION

To administer eyedrops, gently hold the eye open with one hand and drop the medication directly onto the eyeball with the other. Then close the eye to distribute the drops. Let the dog blink several times.

Eye ointment should be applied inside the lower eyelid. Gently pull the eyelid down and out and apply the ointment. Then close the eye and carefully rub to distribute the ointment.

Ear medication may be necessary to clear up an infection, mites or fungus. To apply medication, hold the ear flap up so the canal is visible. Clean as directed by veterinarian (see Chapter 6 for specifics on ear cleaning). Apply drops directly into the ear canal and inside the ear flap if necessary. Then grab the base of the ear with several fingers and massage to distribute the medicine throughout the ear canal. Repeat in the other ear as directed. Most dogs want to shake after having their ears medicated or cleaned, so be sure to stand back!

Squeeze eye ointment into the lower lid.

GERIATRIC DOGS

As Poodles age, they experience significant physical changes. An elderly dog often cannot see, hear or smell as he once did; he may be cranky and less willing to tolerate the excitement of everyday household traffic; he may eat less and gain more weight. Most of these are normal aspects of aging, and you should be aware of these and be willing to accommodate them.

The geriatric dog should receive regular veterinary care to ensure her good health as long as possible. A special diet may be in order to help her aging digestive tract, which no longer works as it should. Vaccinations must be kept current; elderly dogs and puppies are most susceptible to disease. Regular bathing to minimize the "old dog smell" may be necessary.

When your Poodle reaches his "Golden Years," be sure to work closely with your veterinarian. Older dogs have special needs that require attention and kindness.

EUTHANASIA

There are some circumstances in which dogs must be euthanized, which means their lives are humanely brought to an end. Often called "putting a pet to sleep," euthanasia is usually done by a veterinarian by a lethal intravenous injection of an anesthetic agent.

The reason for euthanasia is to end suffering, such as in the case of a severely ill, or very old, dog with no hope of recovery. In addition, dogs of all ages are euthanized at shelters around the United States because there are no homes and owners to accommodate them.

The decision to euthanize a pet is a personal one, though it can be helpful to discuss it with your veterinarian and family members.

Your Happy, Healthy Pet

Your Dog's Name _____

Name on Your Dog's Pedigree (if your dog has one) _____

_____

Where Your Dog Came From _____

_____

Your Dog's Birthday _____

Your Dog's Veterinarian

    Name _____

    Address _____

    Phone Number_____

    Emergency Number_____

Your Dog's Health

    Vaccines

    type _____ date given _____

    type _____ date given _____

    type _____ date given _____

    type _____ date given _____

    Heartworm

    date tested _____ type used_____ start date _____

Your Dog's License Number_____

Groomer's Name and Number _____

Dogsitter/Walker's Name and Number_____

Awards Your Dog Has Won

    Award _____ date earned _____

    Award _____ date earned _____

part three

Enjoying
your
Dog

chapter 8

Basic
Training

by Ian Dunbar, Ph.D., MRCVS

Training is the jewel in the crown—the most important aspect of doggy husbandry. There is no more important variable influencing dog behavior and temperament than the dog's education: A well-trained, well-behaved and good-natured puppydog is always a joy to live with, but an untrained and uncivilized dog can be a perpetual nightmare. Moreover, deny the dog an education and it will not have the opportunity to fulfill its own canine potential; neither will it have the ability to communicate effectively with its human companions.

Luckily, modern psychological training methods are easy, efficient and effective and, above all, considerably dog-friendly and user-friendly. Doggy education is as simple as it is enjoyable. But before you can have a good time play-training with your new dog, you have to learn what to do and how to do it. There is no bigger variable influencing the success of dog training than the *owner's* experience and expertise. *Before you embark on the dog's education, you must first educate yourself.*

Basic Training for Owners

Ideally, basic owner training should begin well *before* you select your dog. Find out all you can about your chosen breed first, then master rudimentary training and handling skills. If you already have your puppy/dog, owner training is a dire emergency—the clock is running! Especially for puppies, the first few weeks at home are the most important and influential days in the dog's life. Indeed, the cause of most adolescent and adult problems may be traced back to the initial days the pup explores his new home. This is the time to establish the *status quo*—to teach the puppy/dog how you would like him to behave and so prevent otherwise quite predictable problems.

In addition to consulting breeders and breed books such as this one (which understandably have a positive breed bias), seek out as many pet owners with your breed you can find. Good points are obvious. What you want to find out are the breed-specific *problems*, so you can nip them in the bud. In particular, you should talk to owners with *adolescent* dogs and make a list of all anticipated problems. Most important, *test drive* at least half a dozen adolescent and adult dogs of your breed yourself. An eight-week-old puppy is deceptively easy to handle, but she will acquire adult size, speed and strength in just four months, so you should learn now what to prepare for.

Puppy and pet dog training classes offer a convenient venue to locate pet owners and observe dogs in action. For a list of suitable trainers in your area, contact the Association of Pet Dog Trainers (see Chapter 13). You may also begin your basic owner training by observing other owners in class. Watch as many classes and test drive as many dogs as possible. Select an upbeat, dog-friendly, people-friendly, fun-and-games, puppydog pet training class to learn the ropes. Also, watch training videos and read training books (see Chapter 12). You must find out what to do and how to do it *before* you have to do it.

Principles of Training

Most people think training comprises teaching the dog to do things such as sit, speak and roll over, but even a four-week-old pup knows how to do these things already. Instead, the first step in training involves teaching the dog human words for each dog behavior and activity and for each aspect of the dog's environment. That way you, the owner, can more easily participate in the dog's domestic education by directing him to perform specific actions appropriately, that is, at the right time, in the right place, and so on. Training opens communication channels, enabling an educated dog to at least understand the owner's requests.

In addition to teaching a dog *what* we want her to do, it is also necessary to teach her *why* she should do what we ask. Indeed, 95 percent of training revolves around motivating the dog *to want to do* what we want. Dogs often understand what their owners want; they just don't see the point of doing it—especially when the owner's repetitively boring and seemingly senseless instructions are totally at odds with much more pressing and exciting doggy distractions. It is not so much the dog who is being stubborn or dominant; rather, it is the owner who has failed to acknowledge the dog's needs and feelings and to approach training from the dog's point of view.

The Meaning of Instructions

The secret to successful training is learning how to use training lures to predict or prompt specific behaviors—to coax the dog to do what you want *when* you want. Any highly valued object (such as a treat or toy) may be used as a lure, which the dog will follow with his eyes and nose. Moving the lure in specific ways entices the dog to move his nose, head and entire body in specific ways. In fact, by learning the art of manipulating various lures, it is possible to teach the dog to assume virtually any body position and perform any action. Once you have control over the expression of the dog's behaviors and can elicit any body position or behavior at will, you can easily teach the dog to perform on request.

Tell your dog what you want him to do, use a lure to entice him to respond correctly, then profusely praise

Teach your dog words for each activity he needs to know, like down.

and maybe reward him once he performs the desired action. For example, verbally request "Fido, sit!" while you move a squeaky toy upwards and backwards over the dog's muzzle (lure-movement and hand signal), smile knowingly as he looks up (to follow the lure) and sits down (as a result of canine anatomical engineering), then praise him to distraction ("Gooood Fido!"). Squeak the toy, offer a training treat and give your dog and yourself a pat on the back.

Being able to elicit desired responses over and over enables the owner to reward the dog over and over. Consequently, the dog begins to think training is fun. For example, the more the dog is rewarded for sitting, the more she enjoys sitting. Eventually the dog comes to realize that, whereas most sitting is appreciated, sitting immediately upon request usually prompts especially enthusiastic praise and a slew of high-level rewards. The dog begins to sit on cue much of the time, showing that she is starting to grasp the meaning of the owner's verbal request and hand signal.

Why Comply?

Most dogs enjoy initial lure/reward training and are only too happy to comply with their owners' wishes. Unfortunately, repetitive drilling without appreciative feedback tends to diminish the dog's enthusiasm until he eventually fails to see the point of complying anymore. Moreover, as the dog approaches adolescence he becomes more easily distracted as he develops other interests. Lengthy sessions with repetitive exercises tend to bore and demotivate both parties. If it's not fun, the owner doesn't do it and neither does the dog.

Integrate training into your dog's life: The greater number of training sessions each day and the *shorter* they are, the more willingly compliant your dog will become. Make sure to have a short (just a few seconds) training interlude before every enjoyable canine activity. For example, ask your dog to sit to greet people, to sit before you throw his Frisbee, and to sit for his supper. Really, sitting is no different from a canine "please." Also, include numerous short training interludes during every enjoyable canine pastime, for example, when playing with the dog or when he is running in the park. In this fashion, doggy distractions may be effectively converted into rewards for training. Just as all games have rules, fun becomes training . . . and training becomes fun.

Eventually, rewards actually become unnecessary to continue motivating your dog. If trained with consideration and kindness, performing the desired behaviors will become self-rewarding and, in a sense, your dog will motivate himself. Just as it is not necessary to reward a human companion during an enjoyable walk in the park, or following a game of tennis, it is hardly necessary to reward our best friend—the dog—for walking by our side or while playing fetch. Human company during enjoyable activities is reward enough for most dogs.

Even though your dog has become self-motivating, it's still good to praise and pet him a lot and offer rewards once in a while, especially for a good job well done. And if for no other reason, praising and rewarding others is good for the human heart.

To train your dog, you need gentle hands, a loving heart and a good attitude.

Punishment

Without a doubt, lure/reward training is by far the best way to teach: Entice your dog to do what you want and then reward him for doing so. Unfortunately, a human shortcoming is to take the good for granted and to moan and groan at the bad. Specifically, the dog's many good behaviors are ignored while the owner focuses on punishing the dog for making mistakes. In extreme cases, instruction is *limited* to punishing mistakes made by a trainee dog, child, employee or husband, even though it has been proven punishment training is notoriously inefficient and ineffective and is decidedly unfriendly and combative. It teaches the dog that training is a drag, almost as quickly as it teaches the dog to dislike his trainer. Why treat our best friends like our worst enemies?

Punishment training is also much more laborious and time consuming. Whereas it takes only a finite amount of time to teach a dog what to chew, for example, it takes much, much longer to punish the dog for each and every mistake. Remember, *there is only one right way!* So why not teach that right way from the outset?!

To make matters worse, punishment training causes severe lapses in the dog's reliability. Since it is obviously impossible to punish the dog each and every time she misbehaves, the dog quickly learns to distinguish between those times when she must comply (so as to avoid impending punishment) and those times when she need not comply, because punishment is impossible. Such times include when the dog is off leash and only six feet away, when the owner is otherwise engaged (talking to a friend, watching television, taking a shower, tending to the baby or chatting on the telephone), or when the dog is left at home alone.

Instances of misbehavior will be numerous when the owner is away, because even when the dog complied in the owner's looming presence, he did so unwillingly. The dog was forced to act against his will, rather than moulding his will to want to please. Hence, when the owner is absent, not only does the dog know he need not comply, he simply does not want to. Again, the trainee is not a stubborn vindictive beast, but rather the trainer has failed to teach.

Punishment training invariably creates unpredictable Jekyll and Hyde behavior.

Trainer's Tools

Many training books extol the virtues of a vast array of training paraphernalia and electronic and metallic gizmos, most of which are designed for canine restraint, correction and punishment, rather than for actual facilitation of doggy education. In reality, most effective training tools are not found in stores; they come from within ourselves. In addition to a willing dog, all you really need is a functional human brain, gentle hands, a loving heart and a good attitude.

In terms of equipment, all dogs do require a quality buckle collar to sport dog tags and to attach the leash (for safety and to comply with local leash laws). Hollow chewtoys (like Kongs or sterilized longbones) and a dog bed or collapsible crate are a must for housetraining. Three additional tools are required:

1. specific lures (training treats and toys) to predict and prompt specific desired behaviors;

2. rewards (praise, affection, training treats and toys) to reinforce for the dog what a lot of fun it all is; and

3. knowledge—how to convert the dog's favorite activities and games (potential distractions to training) into "life-rewards," which may be employed to facilitate training.

The most powerful of these is *knowledge*. Education is the key! Watch training classes, participate in training classes, watch videos, read books, enjoy playtraining with your dog, and then your dog will say "Please," and your dog will say "Thank you!"

Housetraining

If dogs were left to their own devices, certainly they would chew, dig and bark for entertainment and then no doubt highlight a few areas of their living space with sprinkles of urine, in much the same way we decorate by hanging pictures. Consequently, when we ask a dog to live with us, we must teach him *where* he may dig and perform his toilet duties, *what* he may chew and *when* he may bark. After all, when left at home alone for many hours, we cannot expect the dog to amuse himself by completing crosswords or watching the soaps on TV!

Also, it would be decidedly unfair to keep the house rules a secret from the dog, and then get angry and punish the poor critter for inevitably transgressing rules he did not even know existed. Remember, without adequate education and guidance, the dog will be forced to establish his own rules—doggy rules—that most probably will be at odds with the owner's view of domestic living.

Since most problems develop during the first few days the dog is at home, prospective dog owners must be certain they are quite clear about the principles of housetraining *before* they get a dog. Early misbehaviors quickly become established as the status quo—

becoming firmly entrenched as hard-to-break bad habits, which set the precedent for years to come. Make sure to teach your dog good habits right from the start. Good habits are just as hard to break as bad ones!

Ideally, when a new dog comes home, try to arrange for someone to be present for as much as possible during the first few days (for adult dogs) or weeks for puppies. With only a little forethought, it is surprisingly easy to find a puppy sitter, such as a retired person, who would be willing to eat from your refrigerator and watch your television while keeping an eye on the newcomer to encourage the dog to play with chewtoys and to ensure he goes outside on a regular basis.

POTTY TRAINING

To teach the dog where to relieve himself:

1. never let him make a single mistake;
2. let him know where you want him to go; and
3. handsomely reward him for doing so: "GOOOOOOOD DOG!!!" liver treat, liver treat, liver treat!

PREVENTING MISTAKES

A single mistake is a training disaster, since it heralds many more in future weeks. And each time the dog soils the house, this further reinforces the dog's unfortunate preference for an indoor, carpeted toilet. *Do not let an unhousetrained dog have full run of the house if you are away from home or cannot pay full attention.* Instead, confine the dog to an area where elimination is appropriate, such as an outdoor run or, better still, a small, comfortable indoor kennel with access to an outdoor run. When confined in this manner, most dogs will naturally housetrain themselves.

If that's not possible, confine the dog to an area, such as a utility room, kitchen, basement or garage, where elimination may not be desired in the long run but as an interim measure it is certainly preferable to doing it all around the house. Use newspaper to cover the floor of the dog's day room. The newspaper may be used to soak up the urine and to wrap up and dispose of the feces. Once your dog develops a preferred spot for eliminating, it is only necessary to cover that part of the floor with newspaper. The smaller papered area may then be moved (only a little each day) towards the door to the outside. Thus the dog will develop the tendency to go to the door when he needs to relieve himself.

Never confine an unhousetrained dog to a crate for long periods. Doing so would force the dog to soil the crate and ruin its usefulness as an aid for housetraining (see the following discussion).

The first few weeks at home are the most important and influential in your dog's life.

TEACHING WHERE

In order to teach your dog where you would like her to do her business, you have to be there to direct the proceedings—an obvious, yet often neglected, fact of life. In order to be there to teach the dog *where* to go, you need to know *when* she needs to go. Indeed, the success of housetraining depends on the owner's ability to predict these times. Certainly, a regular feeding schedule will facilitate prediction somewhat, but there is nothing like "loading the deck" and influencing the timing of the outcome yourself!

Whenever you are at home, make sure the dog is under constant supervision and/or confined to a small area. If already well trained, simply instruct the dog to lie down in his bed or basket. Alternatively, confine the dog to a crate (doggy den) or tie-down (a short, 18-inch lead that can be clipped to an eye hook in the baseboard). Short-term close confinement strongly inhibits urination and defecation, since the dog does not want to soil his sleeping area. Thus, when you release the puppydog each hour, he will definitely need to urinate immediately and defecate every third or fourth hour. Keep the dog confined to his doggy den and take him to his intended toilet area each hour, every hour, and on the hour.

When taking your dog outside, instruct him to sit quietly before opening the door—he will soon learn to sit by the door when he needs to go out!

TEACHING WHY

Being able to predict when the dog needs to go enables the owner to be on the spot to praise and reward the dog. Each hour, hurry the dog to the intended toilet area in the yard, issue the appropriate instruction ("Go pee!" or "Go poop!"), then give the dog three to four minutes to produce. Praise and offer a couple of training treats when successful. The treats are important because many people fail to praise their dogs with feeling . . . and housetraining is hardly the time for understatement. So either loosen up and enthusiastically praise that dog: "Wuzzzer-wuzzer-wuzzer, hoooser good wuffer den? Hoooo went pee for Daddy?" Or say "Good dog!" as best you can and offer the treats for effect.

Following elimination is an ideal time for a spot of playtraining in the yard or house. Also, an empty dog may be allowed greater freedom around the house for the next half hour or so, just as long as you keep an eye out to make sure he does not get into other kinds of mischief. If you are preoccupied and cannot pay full attention, confine the dog to his doggy den once more to enjoy a peaceful snooze or to play with his many chewtoys.

If your dog does not eliminate within the allotted time outside—no biggie! Back to his doggy den, and then try again after another hour.

As I own large dogs, I always feel more relaxed walking an empty dog, knowing that I will not need to finish our stroll weighted down with bags of feces! Beware of falling into the trap of walking the dog to get it to eliminate. The good ol' dog walk is such an enormous highlight in the dog's life that it represents the single biggest potential reward in domestic dogdom. However, when in a hurry, or during inclement weather, many owners abruptly terminate the walk the moment the dog has done its business. This, in effect, severely punishes the dog for doing the right thing, in the right place at the right time. Consequently, many dogs become strongly inhibited from eliminating outdoors because they know it will signal an abrupt end to an otherwise thoroughly enjoyable walk.

Instead, instruct the dog to relieve himself in the yard prior to going for a walk. If you follow the above instructions, most dogs soon learn to eliminate on cue. As soon as the dog eliminates, praise (and offer a treat or two)—"Good dog! Let's go walkies!" Use the walk as a reward for eliminating in the yard. If the dog does not go, put him back in his doggy den and think about a walk later on. You will find with a "No feces–no walk" policy, your dog will become one of the fastest defecators in the business.

If you do not have a back yard, instruct the dog to eliminate right outside your front door prior to the walk. Not only will this facilitate clean up and disposal of the feces in your own trash can but, also, the walk may again be used as a colossal reward.

Chewing and Barking

Short-term close confinement also teaches the dog that occasional quiet moments are a reality of domestic living. Your puppydog is extremely impressionable during his first few weeks at home. Regular confinement at this time soon exerts a calming influence over the dog's personality. Remember, once the dog is housetrained and calmer, there will be a whole lifetime ahead for the dog to enjoy full run of the house and garden. On the other hand, by letting the newcomer have unrestricted access to the entire household and allowing him to run willy-nilly, he will most certainly develop a bunch of behavior problems in short order, no doubt necessitating confinement later in life. It would not be fair to remedially restrain and confine a dog you have trained, through neglect, to run free.

When confining the dog, make sure he always has an impressive array of suitable chewtoys. Kongs and sterilized longbones (both readily available from pet stores) make the best chewtoys, since they are hollow and may be stuffed with treats to heighten the dog's interest. For example, by stuffing the little hole at the top of a Kong with a small piece of freeze-dried liver, the dog will not want to leave it alone.

Remember, treats do not have to be junk food and they certainly should not represent extra calories. Rather, treats should be part of each dog's regular daily diet:

Make sure your puppy has suitable chewtoys.

Some food may be served in the dog's bowl for breakfast and dinner, some food may be used as training treats, and some food may be used for stuffing chewtoys. I regularly stuff my dogs' many Kongs with different shaped biscuits and kibble. The kibble seems to fall out fairly easily, as do the oval-shaped biscuits, thus rewarding the dog instantaneously for checking out the chewtoys. The bone-shaped biscuits fall out after a while, rewarding the dog for worrying at the chewtoy. But the triangular biscuits never come out. They remain inside the Kong as lures, maintaining the dog's fascination with its chewtoy. To further focus the dog's interest, I always make sure to flavor the triangular biscuits by rubbing them with a little cheese or freeze-dried liver.

If stuffed chewtoys are reserved especially for times the dog is confined, the puppy-dog will soon learn to enjoy quiet moments in her doggy den and she will quickly develop a chewtoy habit—a good habit! This is a simple *passive training* process; all the owner has to do is set up the situation and the dog all but trains herself—easy and effective. Even when the dog is given run of the house, her first inclination will be to indulge her rewarding chewtoy habit rather than destroying less-attractive household articles, such as curtains, carpets, chairs and compact disks. Similarly, a chewtoy chewer will be less inclined to scratch and chew herself excessively. Also, if the dog busies herself as a recreational chewer, she will be less inclined to develop into a recreational barker or digger when left at home alone.

Stuff a number of chewtoys whenever the dog is left confined and remove the extra-special-tasting treats when you return. Your dog will now amuse himself with his chewtoys before falling asleep and then resume playing with his chewtoys when he expects you to return. Since most owner-absent misbehavior happens right after you leave and right before your expected return, your puppydog will now be conveniently preoccupied with his chewtoys at these times.

Come and Sit

Most puppies will happily approach virtually anyone, whether called or not; that is, until they collide with

To teach come, call your dog, open your arms as a welcoming signal, wave a toy or a treat and praise for every step in your direction.

adolescence and develop other more important doggy interests, such as sniffing a multiplicity of exquisite odors on the grass. Your mission, Mr. and/or Ms. Owner, is to teach and reward the pup for coming reliably, willingly and happily when called—and you have just three months to get it done. Unless adequately reinforced, your puppy's tendency to approach people will self-destruct by adolescence.

Call your dog ("Fido, come!"), open your arms (and maybe squat down) as a welcoming signal, waggle a treat or toy as a lure, and reward the puppydog when he comes running. Do not wait to praise the dog until he reaches you—he may come 95 percent of the way and then run off after some distraction. Instead, praise the dog's *first* step towards you and continue praising enthusiastically for *every* step he takes in your direction.

When the rapidly approaching puppy dog is three lengths away from impact, instruct him to sit ("Fido, sit!") and hold the lure in front of you in an outstretched hand to prevent him from hitting you mid-chest and knocking you flat on your back! As Fido decelerates to nose the lure, move the treat upwards and backwards just over his muzzle with an upwards motion of your extended arm (palm-upwards). As the dog looks up to follow the lure, he will sit down (if he jumps up, you are holding the lure too high). Praise the dog for sitting. Move backwards and call him again. Repeat this many times over, always praising when Fido comes and sits; on occasion, reward him.

For the first couple of trials, use a training treat both as a lure to entice the dog to come and sit and as a reward for doing so. Thereafter, try to use different items as lures and rewards. For example, lure the dog with a Kong or Frisbee but reward her with a food treat. Or lure the dog with a food treat but pat her and throw a tennis ball as a reward. After just a few repetitions, dispense with the lures and rewards; the dog will begin to respond willingly to your verbal requests and hand signals just for the prospect of praise from your heart and affection from your hands.

Instruct every family member, friend and visitor how to get the dog to come and sit. Invite people over for a series of pooch parties; do not keep the pup a secret— let other people enjoy this puppy, and let the pup enjoy other people. Puppydog parties are not only fun, they easily attract a lot of people to help *you* train *your* dog. Unless you teach your dog *how* to meet people, that is, to sit for greetings, no doubt the dog will resort to jumping up. Then you and the visitors will get annoyed, and the dog will be punished. This is not fair. *Send out those invitations for puppy parties and teach your dog to be mannerly and socially acceptable.*

Even though your dog quickly masters obedient recalls in the house, his reliability may falter when playing in the back yard or local park. Ironically, it is *the owner* who has unintentionally trained the dog *not* to respond in these instances. By allowing the dog to play and run around and otherwise have a good time, but then to call the dog to put him on leash to take him home, the dog quickly learns playing is fun but training is a drag. Thus, playing in the park becomes a severe distraction, which works against training. Bad news!

Instead, whether playing with the dog off leash or on leash, request him to come at frequent intervals— say, every minute or so. On most occasions, praise and pet the dog for a few seconds while he is sitting, then tell him to go play again. For especially fast recalls, offer a couple of training treats and take the time to praise and pet the dog enthusiastically before releasing him. The dog will learn that coming when called is not necessarily the end of the play session, and neither is it the end of the world; rather, it signals an enjoyable, quality time-out with the owner before resuming play once more. In fact, playing in the park now becomes a very effective life-reward, which works to facilitate training by reinforcing each obedient and timely recall. Good news!

Sit, Down, Stand and Rollover

Teaching the dog a variety of body positions is easy for owner and dog, impressive for spectators and extremely useful for all. Using lure-reward techniques, it is possible to train several positions at once to verbal commands or hand signals (which impress the socks off onlookers).

Sit and *down*—the two control commands—prevent or resolve nearly a hundred behavior problems. For example, if the dog happily and obediently sits or lies down when requested, he cannot jump on visitors, dash out the front door, run around and chase its tail, pester other dogs, harass cats or annoy family, friends or strangers. Additionally, "sit" or "down" are better emergency commands for off-leash control.

It is easier to teach and maintain a reliable sit than maintain a reliable recall. *Sit* is the purest and simplest of commands—either the dog is sitting or he is not. If there is any change of circumstances or potential danger in the park, for example, simply instruct the dog to sit. If he sits, you have a number of options: allow the dog to resume playing when he is safe; walk up and put the dog on leash, or call the dog. The dog will be much more likely to come when called if he has already acknowledged his compliance by sitting. If the dog does not sit in the park—train him to!

Stand and *rollover-stay* are the two positions for examining the dog. Your veterinarian will love you to distraction if you take a little time to teach the dog to stand still and roll over and play possum. Also, your vet bills will be smaller. The rollover-stay is an especially useful command and is really just a variation of the down-stay: whereas the dog lies prone in the traditional down, she lies supine in the rollover-stay.

As with teaching come and sit, the training techniques to teach the dog to assume all other body positions on cue are user-friendly and dog-friendly. Simply give the appropriate request, lure the dog into the desired body position using a training treat or toy and then *praise* (and maybe reward) the dog as soon as he complies. Try not to touch the dog to get him to respond. If you teach the dog by guiding him into position, the dog will quickly learn that rump-pressure means sit, for example, but as yet you still have no control over your dog if he is just six feet away. It will still be necessary to teach the dog to sit on request. So do not make training a time-consuming two-step process; instead, teach the dog to sit to a verbal request or hand signal from the outset. Once the dog sits willingly when requested, by all means use your hands to pet the dog when he does so.

To teach *down* when the dog is already sitting, say "Fido, down!," hold the lure in one hand (palm down) and lower that hand to the floor between the dog's forepaws. As the dog lowers his head to follow the lure, slowly move the lure away from the dog just a fraction (in front of his paws). The dog will lie down as he stretches his nose forward to follow the lure. Praise the dog when he does so. If the dog stands up, you pulled the lure away too far and too quickly.

When teaching the dog to lie down from the standing position, say "down" and lower the lure to the floor as before. Once the dog has lowered his forequarters and assumed a play bow, gently and slowly move the lure *towards* the dog between his forelegs. Praise the dog as soon as his rear end plops down.

After just a couple of trials it will be possible to alternate sits and downs and have the dog energetically perform doggy push-ups. Praise the dog a lot, and after half a dozen or so push-ups reward the dog with a training treat or toy. You will notice the more energetically you move your arm—upwards (palm up) to get the dog to sit, and downwards (palm down) to get the dog to lie down—the more energetically the dog responds to your requests. Now try training the dog in silence and you will notice he has also learned to respond to hand signals. Yeah! Not too shabby for the first session.

To teach *stand* from the sitting position, say "Fido, stand," slowly move the lure half a dog-length away from the dog's nose, keeping it at nose level, and praise the dog as he stands to follow the lure. As soon

Using a food lure to teach sit, down and stand. 1) "Phoenix, Sit." 2) Hand palm upwards, move lure up and back over dog's muzzle. 3) "Good sit, Phoenix!" 4) "Phoenix, down." 5) Hand palm downwards, move lure down to lie between dog's forepaws. 6) "Phoenix, off. Good down, Phoenix!" 7) "Phoenix, sit!" 8) Palm upwards, move lure up and back, keeping it close to dog's muzzle. 9) "Good sit, Phoenix!"

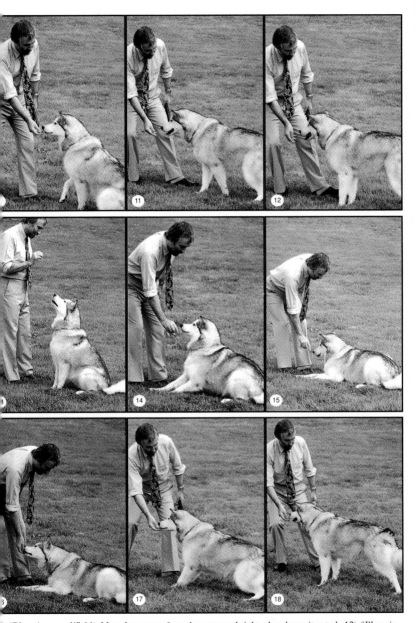

) "Phoenix, stand!" 11) Move lure away from dog at nose height, then lower it a tad. 12) "Phoenix, Good stand, Phoenix!" 13) "Phoenix, down!" 14) Hand palm downwards, move lure down to lie ween dog's forepaws. 15) "Phoenix, off! Good down-stay, Phoenix!" 16) "Phoenix, stand!" 17) Move e away from dog's muzzle up to nose height. 18) "Phoenix, off! Good stand-stay, Phoenix. Now we'll ke the vet and groomer happy!"

as the dog stands, lower the lure to just beneath the dog's chin to entice him to look down; otherwise he will stand and then sit immediately. To prompt the dog to stand from the down position, move the lure half a dog-length upwards and away from the dog, holding the lure at standing nose height from the floor.

Teaching **rollover** is best started from the down position, with the dog lying on one side, or at least with both hind legs stretched out on the same side. Say "Fido, bang!" and move the lure backwards and alongside the dog's muzzle to its elbow (on the side of its outstretched hind legs). Once the dog looks to the side and backwards, very slowly move the lure upwards to the dog's shoulder and backbone. Tickling the dog in the goolies (groin area) often invokes a reflex-raising of the hind leg as an appeasement gesture, which facilitates the tendency to roll over. If you move the lure too quickly and the dog jumps into the standing position, have patience and start again. As soon as the dog rolls onto its back, keep the lure stationary and mesmerize the dog with a relaxing tummy rub.

To teach **rollover-stay** when the dog is standing or moving, say "Fido, bang!" and give the appropriate hand signal (with index finger pointed and thumb cocked in true Sam Spade fashion), then in one fluid movement lure him to first lie down and then rollover-stay as above.

Teaching the dog to **stay** in each of the above four positions becomes a piece of cake after first teaching the dog not to worry at the toy or treat training lure. This is best accomplished by hand feeding dinner kibble. Hold a piece of kibble firmly in your hand and softly instruct "Off!" Ignore any licking and slobbering *for however long the dog worries at the treat*, but say "Take it!" and offer the kibble *the instant* the dog breaks contact with his muzzle. Repeat this a few times, and then up the ante and insist the dog remove his muzzle for one whole second before offering the kibble. Then progressively refine your criteria and have the dog not touch your hand (or treat) for longer and longer periods on each trial, such as for two seconds, four seconds, then six, ten, fifteen, twenty, thirty seconds and so on. The dog soon learns: (1) worrying at the treat never gets results, whereas (2) noncontact is often rewarded after a variable time lapse.

Teaching *"Off!"* has many useful applications in its own right. Additionally, instructing the dog not to touch a training lure often produces spontaneous and magical stays. Request the dog to stand-stay, for example, and not to touch the lure. At first set your sights on a short two-second stay before rewarding the dog. (Remember, every long journey begins with a single step.) However, on subsequent trials, gradually and progressively increase the length of stay required to receive a reward. In no time at all your dog will stand calmly for a minute or so. ·

Relevancy Training

Once you have taught the dog what you expect her to do when requested to come, sit, lie down, stand, rollover and stay, the time is right to teach the dog *why* she should comply with your wishes. The secret is to have many (*many*) extremely short training interludes (two to five seconds each) at numerous (*numerous*) times during the course of the dog's day. Especially work with the dog immediately *before* the dog's good times and *during* the dog's good times. For example, ask your dog to sit and/or lie down each time before opening doors, serving meals, offering treats and tummy rubs; ask the dog to perform a few controlled doggy push-ups before letting her off-leash or throwing a tennis ball; and perhaps request the dog to sit-down-sit-stand-down-stand-rollover before inviting her to cuddle on the couch.

Similarly, request the dog to sit many times during play or on walks, and in no time at all the dog will be only too pleased to follow your instructions because he has learned that a compliant response heralds all sorts of goodies. Basically all you are trying to teach the dog is how to say please: "Please throw the tennis ball. Please may I snuggle on the couch."

Remember, whereas it is important to keep training interludes short, it is equally important to have many short sessions each and every day. The shortest (and most useful) session comprises asking the dog to sit and then go play during a play session. When trained this way, your dog will soon associate training with good times. In fact, the dog may be unable to distinguish between training and good times and, indeed, there should be no distinction. The warped concept that training involves forcing the dog to comply and/or dominating his will is totally at odds with the picture of a truly well-trained dog. In reality, enjoying a game of training with a dog is no different from enjoying a game of backgammon or tennis with a friend; and walking with a dog should be no different from strolling with buddies on the golf course.

Walk by Your Side

Many people attempt to teach a dog to heel by putting him on a leash and physically correcting the dog when he makes mistakes. There are a number of things seriously wrong with this approach, the first being that most people do not want precision heeling; rather, they simply want the dog to follow or walk by their side. Second, when physically restrained during "training," even though the dog may grudgingly mope by your side when "handcuffed" on leash, let's see what happens when he is off leash. History! The dog is in the next county because he never enjoyed walking with you on leash and you have no control over him off leash. So let's just teach the dog off leash from the outset to *want* to walk with us. Third, if the dog has not been trained to heel, it is a trifle hasty to think about punishing the poor dog for making mistakes and breaking heeling rules he didn't even know existed. This is simply not fair! Surely, if the dog had been adequately taught how to heel, he would seldom make mistakes and hence there would be no need to correct the dog. Remember, each mistake and each correction (punishment) advertise the trainer's inadequacy, not the dog's. The dog is not stubborn, he is not stupid and he is not bad. Even if he were, he would still require training, so let's train him properly.

Let's teach the dog to *enjoy* following us and to *want* to walk by our side offleash. Then it will be easier to teach high-precision off-leash heeling patterns if desired. After attaching the leash for safety on outdoor walks, but before going anywhere, it is necessary to teach the dog specifically not to pull. Now it will be much easier to teach on-leash walking and heeling because the dog already wants to walk with you, he is familiar with the desired walking and heeling positions and he knows not to pull.

FOLLOWING

Start by training your dog to follow you. Many puppies will follow if you simply walk away from them and maybe click your fingers or chuckle. Adult dogs may require additional enticement to stimulate them to follow, such as a training lure or, at the very least, a lively trainer. To teach the dog to follow: (1) keep walking and (2) walk away from the dog. If the dog attempts to lead or lag, change pace; slow down if the dog forges too far ahead, but speed up if he lags too far behind. Say "Steady!" or "Easy!" each time before you slow down and "Quickly!" or "Hustle!" each time before you speed up, and the dog will learn to change pace on cue. If the dog lags or leads too far, or if he wanders right or left, simply walk quickly in the opposite direction and maybe even run away from the dog and hide.

Practicing is a lot of fun; you can set up a course in your home, yard or park to do this. Indoors, entice the dog to follow upstairs, into a bedroom, into the bathroom, downstairs, around the living room couch, zigzagging between dining room chairs and into the kitchen for dinner. Outdoors, get the dog to follow around park benches, trees, shrubs and along walkways and lines in the grass. (For safety outdoors, it is advisable to attach a long line on the dog, but never exert corrective tension on the line.)

Remember, following has a lot to do with attitude—*your* attitude! Most probably your dog will *not* want to follow Mr. Grumpy Troll with the personality of wilted lettuce. Lighten up—walk with a jaunty step, whistle a happy tune, sing, skip and tell jokes to your dog and he will be right there by your side.

BY YOUR SIDE

It is smart to train the dog to walk close on one side or the other—either side will do, your choice. When walking, jogging or cycling, it is generally bad news to have the dog suddenly cut in front of you. In fact, I train my dogs to walk "By my side" and "Other side"—both very useful instructions. It is possible to position the dog fairly accurately by looking to the appropriate side and clicking your fingers or slapping your thigh on that side. A precise positioning may be attained by holding a training lure, such as a chewtoy, tennis ball, or food treat. Stop and stand still several times throughout the walk, just as you would when window shopping or meeting a friend. Use the lure to make sure the dog slows down and stays close whenever you stop.

When teaching the dog to heel, we generally want her to sit in heel position when we stop. Teach heel

Using a toy to teach sit-heel-sit sequences: 1) "Phoenix, heel!" Standing still, move lure up and back over dog's muzzle.... 2) To position dog sitting in heel position on your left side. 3) "Phoenix, heel!" wagging lure in left hand. Change lure to right hand in preparation for sit signal.

122

position at the standstill and the dog will learn that the default heel position is sitting by your side (left or right—your choice, unless you wish to compete in obedience trials, in which case the dog must heel on the left).

Several times a day, stand up and call your dog to come and sit in heel position—"Fido, heel!" For example, instruct the dog to come to heel each time there are commercials on TV, or each time you turn a page of a novel, and the dog will get it in a single evening.

Practice straight-line heeling and turns separately. With the dog sitting at heel, teach him to turn in place. After each quarter-turn, half-turn or full turn in place, lure the dog to sit at heel. Now it's time for short straight-line heeling sequences, no more than a few steps at a time. Always think of heeling in terms of Sit-Heel-Sit sequences—start and end with the dog in position and do your best to keep him there when moving. Progressively increase the number of steps in each sequence. When the dog remains close for 20 yards of straight-line heeling, it is time to add a few turns and then sign up for a happy-heeling obedience class to get some advice from the experts.

4) Use hand signal only to lure dog to sit as you stop. Eventually, dog will sit automatically at heel whenever you stop. 5) "Good dog!"

No Pulling on Leash

You can start teaching your dog not to pull on leash anywhere—in front of the television or outdoors—but regardless of location, you must not take a single step with tension in the leash. For a reason known only to dogs, even just a couple of paces of pulling on leash is intrinsically motivating and diabolically rewarding. Instead, attach the leash to the dog's collar, grasp the other end firmly with both hands held close to your chest, and stand still—do not budge an inch. Have somebody watch you with a stopwatch to time your progress, or else you will never believe this will work and so you will not even try the exercise, and your shoulder and the dog's neck will be traumatized for years to come.

Stand still and wait for the dog to stop pulling, and to sit and/or lie down. All dogs stop pulling and sit eventually. Most take only a couple of minutes; the all-time record is 22 $\frac{1}{5}$ minutes. Time how long it takes. Gently praise the dog when he stops pulling, and as soon as he sits, enthusiastically praise the dog and take just one step forwards, then immediately stand still. This single step usually demonstrates the ballistic reinforcing nature of pulling on leash; most dogs explode to the end of the leash, so be prepared for the strain. Stand firm and wait for the dog to sit again. Repeat this half a dozen times and you will probably notice a progressive reduction in the force of the dog's one-step explosions and a radical reduction in the time it takes for the dog to sit each time.

As the dog learns "Sit we go" and "Pull we stop," she will begin to walk forward calmly with each single step and automatically sit when you stop. Now try two steps before you stop. Wooooooo! Scary! When the dog has mastered two steps at a time, try for three. After each success, progressively increase the number of steps in the sequence: try four steps and then six, eight, ten and twenty steps before stopping. Congratulations! You are now walking the dog on leash.

Whenever walking with the dog (off leash or on leash), make sure you stop periodically to practice a few position commands and stays before instructing the dog to "Walk on!" (Remember, you want the dog to be compliant everywhere, not just in the kitchen when his dinner is at hand.) For example, stopping every 25 yards to briefly train the dog amounts to over 200 training interludes within a single three-mile stroll. And each training session is in a different location. You will not believe the improvement within just the first mile of the first walk.

To put it another way, integrating training into a walk offers 200 separate opportunities to use the continuance of the walk as a reward to reinforce the dog's education. Moreover, some training interludes may comprise continuing education for the dog's walking skills: Alternate short periods of the dog walking calmly by your side with periods when the dog is allowed to sniff and investigate the environment. Now sniffing odors on the grass and meeting other dogs become rewards which reinforce the dog's calm and mannerly demeanor. Good Lord! Whatever next? Many enjoyable walks together of course. Happy trails!

THE IMPORTANCE OF TRICKS

Nothing will improve a dog's quality of life better than having a few tricks under its belt. Teaching any trick expands the dog's vocabulary, which facilitates communication and improves the owner's control. Also, specific tricks help prevent and resolve specific behavior problems. For example, by teaching the dog to fetch his toys, the dog learns carrying a toy makes the owner happy and, therefore, will be more likely to chew his toy than other inappropriate items.

More important, teaching tricks prompts owners to lighten up and train with a sunny disposition. Really, tricks should be no different from any other behaviors we put on cue. But they are. When teaching tricks, owners have a much sweeter attitude, which in turn motivates the dog and improves her willingness to comply. The dog feels tricks are a blast, but formal commands are a drag. In fact, tricks are so enjoyable, they may be used as rewards in training by asking the dog to come, sit and down-stay and then rollover for a tummy rub. Go on, try it: Crack a smile and even giggle when the dog promptly and willingly lies down and stays.

Most important, performing tricks prompts onlookers to smile and giggle. Many people are scared of dogs, especially large ones. And nothing can be more off-putting for a dog than to be constantly confronted by strangers who don't like him because of his size or the way he looks. Uneasy people put the dog on edge, causing him to back off and bark, only frightening people all the more. And so a vicious circle develops, with the people's fear fueling the dog's fear *and vice versa*. Instead, tie a pink ribbon to your dog's collar and practice all sorts of tricks on walks and in the park, and you will be pleasantly amazed how it changes people's attitudes toward your friendly dog. The dog's repertoire of tricks is limited only by the trainer's imagination. Below I have described three of my favorites:

SPEAK AND SHUSH

The training sequence involved in teaching a dog to bark on request is no different from that used when training any behavior on cue: request—lure—response—reward. As always, the secret of success lies in finding an effective lure. If the dog always barks at the doorbell, for example, say "Rover, speak!", have an accomplice ring the doorbell, then reward the dog for barking. After a few woofs, ask Rover to "Shush!", waggle a food treat under his nose (to entice him to sniff and thus to shush), praise him when quiet and eventually offer the treat as a reward. Alternate "Speak" and "Shush," progressively increasing the length of shush-time between each barking bout.

PLAYBOW

With the dog standing, say "Bow!" and lower the food lure (palm upwards) to rest between the dog's forepaws. Praise as the dog lowers her forequarters and sternum to the ground (as when teaching the down), but then lure the dog to stand and offer the treat. On successive trials, gradually increase the length of time the dog is required to remain in the playbow posture in order to gain a food reward. If the dog's rear end collapses into a down, say nothing and offer no reward; simply start over.

BE A BEAR

With the dog sitting backed into a corner to prevent him from toppling over backwards, say "Be a Bear!" With bent paw and palm down, raise a lure upwards and backwards along the top of the dog's muzzle. Praise the dog when he sits up on his haunches and offer the treat as a reward. To prevent the dog from standing on his hind legs, keep the lure closer to the dog's muzzle. On each trial, progressively increase the length of time the dog is required to sit up to receive a food reward. Since lure/reward training is so easy, teach the dog to stand and walk on his hind legs as well!

Teaching "Be a Bear"

chapter 9

Getting
Active
with your Dog

by Bardi McLennan

Once you and your dog have graduated from basic obedience training and are beginning to work together as a team, you can take part in the growing world of dog activities. There are so many fun things to do with your dog! Just remember, people and dogs don't always learn at the same pace, so don't be upset if you (or your dog) need more than two basic training courses before your team becomes operational. Even smart dogs don't go straight to college from kindergarten!

Just as there are events geared to certain types of dogs, so there are ones that are more appealing to certain types of people. In some

128

activities, you give the commands and your dog does the work (upland game hunting is one example), while in others, such as agility, you'll both get a workout. You may want to aim for prestigious titles to add to your dog's name, or you may want nothing more than the sheer enjoyment of being around other people and their dogs. Passive or active, participation has its own rewards.

Consider your dog's physical capabilities when looking into any of the canine activities. It's easy to see that a Basset Hound is not built for the racetrack, nor would a Chihuahua be the breed of choice for pulling a sled. A loyal dog will attempt almost anything you ask him to do, so it is up to you to know your dog's limitations. A dog must be physically sound in order to compete at any level in athletic activities, and being mentally sound is a definite plus. Advanced age, however, may not be a deterrent. Many dogs still hunt and herd at ten or twelve years of age. It's entirely possible for dogs to be "fit at 50." Take your dog for a checkup, explain to your vet the type of activity you have in mind and be guided by his or her findings.

All dogs seem to love playing flyball.

You needn't be restricted to breed-specific sports if it's only fun you're after. Certain AKC activities are limited to designated breeds; however, as each new trial, test or sport has grown in popularity, so has the variety of breeds encouraged to participate at a fun level.

But don't shortchange your fun, or that of your dog, by thinking only of the basic function of her breed. Once a dog has learned how to learn, she can be taught to do just about anything as long as the size of the dog is right for the job and you both think it is fun and rewarding. In other words, you are a team.

To get involved in any of the activities detailed in this chapter, look for the names and addresses of the organizations that sponsor them in Chapter 13. You can also ask your breeder or a local dog trainer for contacts.

You can compete in obedience trials with a well trained dog.

Official American Kennel Club Activities

The following tests and trials are some of the events sanctioned by the AKC and sponsored by various dog clubs. Your dog's expertise will be rewarded with impressive titles. You can participate just for fun, or be competitive and go for those awards.

OBEDIENCE

Training classes begin with pups as young as three months of age in kindergarten puppy training, then advance to pre-novice (all exercises on lead) and go on to novice, which is where you'll start off-lead work. In obedience classes dogs learn to sit, stay, heel and come through a variety of exercises. Once you've got the basics down, you can enter obedience trials and work toward earning your dog's first degree, a C.D. (Companion Dog).

The next level is called "Open," in which jumps and retrieves perk up the dog's interest. Passing grades in competition at this level earn a C.D.X. (Companion Dog Excellent). Beyond that lies the goal of the most ambitious—Utility (U.D. and even U.D.X. or OTCh, an Obedience Champion).

AGILITY

All dogs can participate in the latest canine sport to have gained worldwide popularity for its fun and excitement, agility. It began in England as a canine version of horse show-jumping, but because dogs are more agile and able to perform on verbal commands, extra feats were added such as climbing, balancing and racing through tunnels or in and out of weave poles. Many of the obstacles (regulation or homemade) can be set up in your own backyard. If the agility bug bites, you could end up in international competition!

For starters, your dog should be obedience trained, even though, in the beginning, the lessons may all be taught on lead. Once the dog understands the commands (and you do, too), it's as easy as guiding the dog over a prescribed course, one obstacle at a time. In competition, the race is against the clock, so wear your running shoes! The dog starts with 200 points and the judge deducts for infractions and misadventures along the way.

All dogs seem to love agility and respond to it as if they were being turned loose in a playground paradise. Your dog's enthusiasm will be contagious; agility turns into great fun for dog and owner.

FIELD TRIALS AND HUNTING TESTS

There are field trials and hunting tests for the sporting breeds—retrievers, spaniels and pointing breeds, and for some hounds—Bassets, Beagles and Dachshunds. Field trials are competitive events that test a dog's ability to perform the functions for which she was bred. Hunting tests, which are open to retrievers,

---

TITLES AWARDED BY THE AKC

Conformation: Ch. (Champion)

Obedience: CD (Companion Dog); CDX (Companion Dog Excellent); UD (Utility Dog); UDX (Utility Dog Excellent); OTCh. (Obedience Trial Champion)

Field: JH (Junior Hunter); SH (Senior Hunter); MH (Master Hunter); AFCh. (Amateur Field Champion); FCh. (Field Champion)

Lure Coursing: JC (Junior Courser); SC (Senior Courser)

Herding: HT (Herding Tested); PT (Pre-Trial Tested); HS (Herding Started); HI (Herding Intermediate); HX (Herding Excellent); HCh. (Herding Champion)

Tracking: TD (Tracking Dog); TDX (Tracking Dog Excellent)

Agility: NAD (Novice Agility); OAD (Open Agility); ADX (Agility Excellent); MAX (Master Agility)

Earthdog Tests: JE (Junior Earthdog); SE (Senior Earthdog); ME (Master Earthdog)

Canine Good Citizen: CGC

Combination: DC (Dual Champion—Ch. and Fch.); TC (Triple Champion—Ch., Fch., and OTCh.)

131

spaniels and pointing breeds only, are noncompetitive and are a means of judging the dog's ability as well as that of the handler.

Hunting is a very large and complex part of canine sports, and if you own one of the breeds that hunts, the events are a great treat for your dog and you. He gets to do what he was bred for, and you get to work with him and watch him do it. You'll be proud of and amazed at what your dog can do.

Fortunately, the AKC publishes a series of booklets on these events, which outline the rules and regulations and include a glossary of the sometimes complicated terms. The AKC also publishes newsletters for field trialers and hunting test enthusiasts. The United Kennel Club (UKC) also has informative materials for the hunter and his dog.

Retrievers and other sporting breeds get to do what they're bred to in hunting tests.

HERDING TESTS AND TRIALS

Herding, like hunting, dates back to the first known uses man made of dogs. The interest in herding today is widespread, and if you own a herding breed, you can join in the activity. Herding dogs are tested for their natural skills to keep a flock of ducks, sheep or cattle together. If your dog shows potential, you can start at the testing level, where your dog can earn a title for showing an inherent herding ability. With training you can advance to the trial level, where your dog should be capable of controlling even difficult livestock in diverse situations.

LURE COURSING

The AKC Tests and Trials for Lure Coursing are open to traditional sighthounds—Greyhounds, Whippets,

Borzoi, Salukis, Afghan Hounds, Ibizan Hounds and Scottish Deerhounds—as well as to Basenjis and Rhodesian Ridgebacks. Hounds are judged on overall ability, follow, speed, agility and endurance. This is possibly the most exciting of the trials for spectators, because the speed and agility of the dogs is awesome to watch as they chase the lure (or "course") in heats of two or three dogs at a time.

TRACKING

Tracking is another activity in which almost any dog can compete because every dog that sniffs the ground when taken outdoors is, in fact, tracking. The hard part comes when the rules as to what, when and where the dog tracks are determined by a person, not the dog! Tracking tests cover a large area of fields, woods and roads. The tracks are laid hours before the dogs go to work on them, and include "tricks" like cross-tracks and sharp turns. If you're interested in search-and-rescue work, this is the place to start.

This tracking dog is hot on the trail.

EARTHDOG TESTS FOR SMALL TERRIERS AND DACHSHUNDS

These tests are open to Australian, Bedlington, Border, Cairn, Dandie Dinmont, Smooth and Wire Fox, Lakeland, Norfolk, Norwich, Scottish, Sealyham, Skye, Welsh and West Highland White Terriers as well as Dachshunds. The dogs need no prior training for this terrier sport. There is a qualifying test on the day of the event, so dog and handler learn the rules on the spot. These tests, or "digs," sometimes end with informal races in the late afternoon.

Here are some of the extracurricular obedience and racing activities that are not regulated by the AKC or UKC, but are generally run by clubs or a group of dog fanciers and are often open to all.

Canine Freestyle This activity is something new on the scene and is variously likened to dancing, dressage or ice skating. It is meant to show the athleticism of the dog, but also requires showmanship on the part of the dog's handler. If you and your dog like to ham it up for friends, you might want to look into freestyle.

Lure coursing lets sighthounds do what they do best—run!

Scent Hurdle Racing Scent hurdle racing is purely a fun activity sponsored by obedience clubs with members forming competing teams. The height of the hurdles is based on the size of the shortest dog on the team. On a signal, one team dog is released on each of two side-by-side courses and must clear every hurdle before picking up its own dumbbell from a platform and returning over the jumps to the handler. As each dog returns, the next on that team is sent. Of course, that is what the dogs are supposed to do. When the dogs improvise (going under or around the hurdles, stealing another dog's dumbbell, and so forth), it no doubt frustrates the handlers, but just adds to the fun for everyone else.

Flyball This type of racing is similar, but after negotiating the four hurdles, the dog comes to a flyball box, steps on a lever that releases a tennis ball into the air, catches the ball and returns over the hurdles to the starting point. This game also becomes extremely fun for spectators because the dogs sometimes cheat by catching a ball released by the dog in the next lane. Three titles can be earned—Flyball Dog (F.D.), Flyball Dog Excellent (F.D.X.) and Flyball Dog Champion (Fb.D.Ch.)—all awarded by the North American Flyball Association, Inc.

Dogsledding The name conjures up the Rocky Mountains or the frigid North, but you can find dogsled clubs in such unlikely spots as Maryland, North Carolina and Virginia! Dogsledding is primarily for the Nordic breeds such as the Alaskan Malamutes, Siberian Huskies and Samoyeds, but other breeds can try. There are some practical backyard applications to this sport, too. With parental supervision, almost any strong dog could pull a child's sled.

Coming over the A-frame on an agility course.

These are just some of the many recreational ways you can get to know and understand your multifaceted dog better and have fun doing it.

chapter 10

Your Dog

and your

Family

by Bardi McLennan

Adding a dog automatically increases your family by one, no matter whether you live alone in an apartment or are part of a mother, father and six kids household. The single-person family is fair game for numerous and varied canine misconceptions as to who is dog and who pays the bills, whereas a dog in a houseful of children will consider himself to be just one of the gang, littermates all. One dog and one child may give a dog reason to believe they are both kids or both dogs. Either interpretation requires parental supervision and sometimes speedy intervention.

As soon as one paw goes through the door into your home, Rufus (or Rufina) has to make many adjustments to become a part of your family. Your job is to make him fit in as painlessly as possible. An older dog may have some frame of reference from past experience, but to a 10-week-old puppy, everything is brand new: people, furniture, stairs, when and where people eat, sleep or watch TV, his own place and everyone else's space, smells, sounds, outdoors—everything!

Puppies, and newly acquired dogs of any age, do not need what we think of as "freedom." If you leave a new dog or puppy loose in the house, you will almost certainly return to chaotic destruction and the dog will forever after equate your homecoming with a time of punishment to be dreaded. It is unfair to give your dog what amounts to "freedom to get into trouble." Instead, confine him to a crate for brief periods of your absence (up to three or four hours) and, for the long haul, a workday for example, confine him to one untrashable area with his own toys, a bowl of water and a radio left on (low) in another room.

Lots of pets get along with each other just fine.

For the first few days, when not confined, put Rufus on a long leash tied to your wrist or waist. This umbilical cord method enables the dog to learn all about you from your body language and voice, and to learn by his own actions which things in the house are NO! and which ones are rewarded by "Good dog." Housetraining will be easier with the pup always by your side. Speaking of which, accidents do happen. That goal of "completely housetrained" takes up to a year, or the length of time it takes the pup to mature.

The All-Adult Family

Most dogs in an adults-only household today are likely to be latchkey pets, with no one home all day but the dog. When you return after a tough day on the job, the dog can and should be your relaxation therapy. But going home can instead be a daily frustration.

Separation anxiety is a very common problem for the dog in a working household. It may begin with whines and barks of loneliness, but it will soon escalate into a frenzied destruction derby. That is why it is so important to set aside the time to teach a dog to relax when left alone in his confined area and to understand that he can trust you to return.

Let the dog get used to your work schedule in easy stages. Confine him to one room and go in and out of that room over and over again. Be casual about it. No physical, voice or eye contact. When the pup no longer even notices your comings and goings, leave the house for varying lengths of time, returning to stay home for a few minutes and gradually increasing the time away. This training can take days, but the dog is learning that you haven't left him forever and that he can trust you.

Any time you leave the dog, but especially during this training period, be casual about your departure. No anxiety-building fond farewells. Just "Bye" and go! Remember the "Good dog" when you return to find everything more or less as you left it.

If things are a mess (or even a disaster) when you return, greet the dog, take him outside to eliminate, and then put him in his crate while you clean up. Rant and rave in the shower! *Do not* punish the dog. You were not there when it happened, and the rule is: Only punish as you catch the dog in the act of wrongdoing. Obviously, it makes sense to get your latchkey puppy when you'll have a week or two to spend on these training essentials.

Family weekend activities should include Rufus whenever possible. Depending on the pup's age, now is the time for a long walk in the park, playtime in the backyard, a hike in the woods. Socializing is as important as health care, good food and physical exercise, so visiting Aunt Emma or Uncle Harry and the next-door neighbor's dog or cat is essential to developing an outgoing, friendly temperament in your pet.

If you are a single adult, socializing Rufus at home and away will prevent him from becoming overly protective of you (or just overly attached) and will also prevent such behavioral problems as dominance or fear of strangers.

Babies

Whether already here or on the way, babies figure larger than life in the eyes of a dog. If the dog is there first, let him in on all your baby preparations in the house. When baby arrives, let Rufus sniff any item of clothing that has been on the baby before Junior comes home. Then let Mom greet the dog first before introducing the new family member. Hold the baby down for the dog to see and sniff, but make sure someone's holding the dog on lead in case of any sudden moves. Don't play keep-away or tease the dog with the baby, which only invites undesirable jumping up.

The dog and the baby are "family," and for starters can be treated almost as equals. Things rapidly change, however, especially when baby takes to creeping around on all fours on the dog's turf or, better yet, has yummy pudding all over her face and hands! That's when a lot of things in the dog's and baby's lives become more separate than equal.

Dogs are perfect confidants.

Toddlers make terrible dog owners, but if you can't avoid the combination, use patient discipline (that is, positive teaching rather than punishment), and use time-outs before you run out of patience.

A dog and a baby (or toddler, or an assertive young child) should never be left alone together. Take the dog with you or confine him. With a baby or youngsters in the house, you'll have plenty of use for that wonderful canine safety device called a crate!

Young Children

Any dog in a house with kids will behave pretty much as the kids do, good or bad. But even good dogs and good children can get into trouble when play becomes rowdy and active.

Teach children how to play nicely with a puppy.

Legs bobbing up and down, shrill voices screeching, a ball hurtling overhead, all add up to exuberant frustration for a dog who's just trying to be part of the gang. In a pack of puppies, any legs or toys being chased would be caught by a set of teeth, and all the pups involved would understand that is how the game is played. Kids do not understand this, nor do parents tolerate it. Bring Rufus indoors before you have reason to regret it. This is time-out, not a punishment.

You can explain the situation to the children and tell them they must play quieter games until the puppy learns not to grab them with his mouth. Unfortunately, you can't explain it that easily to the dog. With adult supervision, they will learn how to play together.

Young children love to tease. Sticking their faces or wiggling their hands or fingers in the dog's face is teasing. To another person it might be just annoying, but it is threatening to a dog. There's another difference: We can make the child stop by an explanation, but the only way a dog can stop it is with a warning growl and then with teeth. Teasing is the major cause of children being bitten by their pets. Treat it seriously.

140

Older Children

The best age for a child to get a first dog is between the ages of 8 and 12. That's when kids are able to accept some real responsibility for their pet. Even so, take the child's vow of "I will never *ever* forget to feed (brush, walk, etc.) the dog" for what it's worth: a child's good intention at that moment. Most kids today have extra lessons, soccer practice, Little League, ballet, and so forth piled on top of school schedules. There will be many times when Mom will have to come to the dog's rescue. "I walked the dog for you so you can set the table for me" is one way to get around a missed appointment without laying on blame or guilt.

Kids in this age group make excellent obedience trainers because they are into the teaching/learning process themselves and they lack the self-consciousness of adults. Attending a dog show is something the whole family can enjoy, and watching Junior Showmanship may catch the eye of the kids. Older children can begin to get involved in many of the recreational activities that were reviewed in the previous chapter. Some of the agility obstacles, for example, can be set up in the backyard as a family project (with an adult making sure all the equipment is safe and secure for the dog).

Older kids are also beginning to look to the future, and may envision themselves as veterinarians or trainers or show dog handlers or writers of the next Lassie best-seller. Dogs are perfect confidants for these dreams. They won't tell a soul.

Other Pets

Introduce all pets tactfully. In a dog/cat situation, hold the dog, not the cat. Let two dogs meet on neutral turf—a stroll in the park or a walk down the street—with both on loose leads to permit all the normal canine ways of saying hello, including routine sniffing, circling, more sniffing, and so on. Small creatures such as hamsters, chinchillas or mice must be kept safe from their natural predators (dogs and cats).

Festive Family Occasions

Parties are great for people, but not necessarily for puppies. Until all the guests have arrived, put the dog in his crate or in a room where he won't be disturbed. A socialized dog can join the fun later as long as he's not underfoot, annoying guests or into the hors d'oeuvres.

There are a few dangers to consider, too. Doors opening and closing can allow a puppy to slip out unnoticed in the confusion, and you'll be organizing a search party instead of playing host or hostess. Party food and buffet service are not for dogs. Let Rufus party in his crate with a nice big dog biscuit.

At Christmas time, not only are tree decorations dangerous and breakable (and perhaps family heirlooms), but extreme caution should be taken with the lights, cords and outlets for the tree lights and any other festive lighting. Occasionally a dog lifts a leg, ignoring the fact that the tree is indoors. To avoid this, use a canine repellent, made for gardens, on the tree. Or keep him out of the tree room unless supervised. And whatever you do, *don't* invite trouble by hanging his toys on the tree!

Car Travel

Before you plan a vacation by car or RV with Rufus, be sure he enjoys car travel. Nothing spoils a holiday quicker than a carsick dog! Work within the dog's comfort level. Get in the car with the dog in his crate or attached to a canine car safety belt and just sit there until he relaxes. That's all. Next time, get in the car, turn on the engine and go nowhere. Just sit. When that is okay, turn on the engine and go around the block. Now you can go for a ride and include a stop where you get out, leaving the dog for a minute or two.

On a warm day, always park in the shade and leave windows open several inches. And return quickly. It only takes 10 minutes for a car to become an overheated steel death trap.

Motel or Pet Motel?

Not all motels or hotels accept pets, but you have a much better choice today than even a few years ago. To find a dog-friendly lodging, look at *On the Road Again With Man's Best Friend*, a series of directories that detail bed and breakfasts, inns, family resorts and other hotels/motels. Some places require a refundable deposit to cover any damage incurred by the dog. More B&Bs accept pets now, but some restrict the size.

If taking Rufus with you is not feasible, check out boarding kennels in your area. Your veterinarian may offer this service, or recommend a kennel or two he or she is familiar with. Go see the facilities for yourself, ask about exercise, diet, housing, and so on. Or, if you'd rather have Rufus stay home, look into bonded petsitters, many of whom will also bring in the mail and water your plants.

chapter 11

Your Dog
and your
Community

by Bardi McLennan

Step outside your home with your dog and you are no longer just family, you are both part of your community. This is when the phrase "responsible pet ownership" takes on serious implications. For starters, it means you pick up after your dog—not just occasionally, but every time your dog eliminates away from home. That means you have joined the Plastic Baggy Brigade! You always have plastic sandwich bags in your pocket and several in the car. It means you teach your kids how to use them, too. If you think this is "yucky," just imagine what

the person (a non-doggy person) who inadvertently steps in the mess thinks!

Your responsibility extends to your neighbors: To their ears (no annoying barking); to their property (their garbage, their lawn, their flower beds, their cat— especially their cat); to their kids (on bikes, at play); to their kids' toys and sports equipment.

There are numerous dog-related laws, ranging from simple dog licensing and leash laws to those holding you liable for any physical injury or property damage done by your dog. These laws are in place to protect everyone in the community, including you and your dog. There are town ordinances and state laws which are by no means the same in all towns or all states. Ignorance of the law won't get you off the hook. The time to find out what the laws are where you live is now.

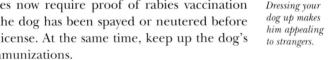

Be sure your dog's license is current. This is not just a good local ordinance, it can make the difference between finding your lost dog or not. Many states now require proof of rabies vaccination and that the dog has been spayed or neutered before issuing a license. At the same time, keep up the dog's annual immunizations.

Dressing your dog up makes him appealing to strangers.

Never let your dog run loose in the neighborhood. This will not only keep you on the right side of the leash law, it's the outdoor version of the rule about not giving your dog "freedom to get into trouble."

Good Canine Citizen

Sometimes it's hard for a dog's owner to assess whether or not the dog is sufficiently socialized to be accepted by the community at large. Does Rufus or Rufina display good, controlled behavior in public? The AKC's Canine Good Citizen program is available through many dog organizations. If your dog passes the test, the title "CGC" is earned.

The overall purpose is to turn your dog into a good neighbor and to teach you about your responsibility to your community as a dog owner. Here are the ten things your dog must do willingly:

1. Allow a stranger to handle him or her as a groomer or veterinarian would.
2. Accept a stranger stopping to chat with you.
3. Walk nicely on a loose lead.
4. Walk calmly through a crowd.
5. Sit and be petted by a stranger.
6. Sit and down on command.
7. Stay put when you move away.
8. Casually greet another dog.
9. React confidently to distractions.
10. Accept being tied up in a strange place and left alone for a few minutes.

Schools and Dogs

Schools are getting involved with pet ownership on an educational level. It has been proven that children who are kind to animals are humane in their attitude toward other people as adults.

A dog is a child's best friend, and so children are often primary pet owners, if not the primary caregivers. Unfortunately, they are also the ones most often bitten by dogs. This occurs due to a lack of understanding that pets, no matter how sweet, cuddly and loving, are still animals. Schools, along with parents, dog clubs, dog fanciers and the AKC, are working to change all that with video programs for children not only in grade school, but in the nursery school and pre-kindergarten age group. Teaching youngsters how to be responsible dog owners is important community work. When your dog has a CGC, volunteer to take part in an educational classroom event put on by your dog club.

Boy Scout Merit Badge

A Merit Badge for Dog Care can be earned by any Boy Scout ages 11 to 18. The requirements are not easy, but amount to a complete course in responsible dog care and general ownership. Here are just a few of the things a Scout must do to earn that badge:

Point out ten parts of the dog using the correct names.

Give a report (signed by parent or guardian) on your care of the dog (feeding, food used, housing, exercising, grooming and bathing), plus what has been done to keep the dog healthy.

Explain the right way to obedience train a dog, and demonstrate three comments.

Several of the requirements have to do with health care, including first aid, handling a hurt dog, and the dangers of home treatment for a serious ailment.

The final requirement is to know the local laws and ordinances involving dogs.

There are similar programs for Girl Scouts and 4-H members.

Local Clubs

Local dog clubs are no longer in existence just to put on a yearly dog show. Today, they are apt to be the hub of the community's involvement with pets. Dog clubs conduct educational forums with big-name speakers, stage demonstrations of canine talent in a busy mall and take dogs of various breeds to schools for class-room discussion.

The quickest way to feel accepted as a member in a club is to volunteer your services! Offer to help with something—anything—and watch your popularity (and your interest) grow.

Therapy Dogs

Once your dog has earned that essential CGC and reliably demonstrates a steady, calm temperament, you could look into what therapy dogs are doing in your area.

Therapy dogs go with their owners to visit patients at hospitals or nursing homes, generally remaining on leash but able to coax a pat from a stiffened hand, a smile from a blank face, a few words from sealed lips or a hug from someone in need of love.

Nursing homes cover a wide range of patient care. Some specialize in care of the elderly, some in the treatment of specific illnesses, some in physical therapy. Children's facilities also welcome visits from trained therapy dogs for boosting morale in their pediatric patients. Hospice care for the terminally ill and the at-home care of AIDS patients are other areas where this canine visiting is desperately needed. Therapy dog training comes first.

Your dog can make a difference in lots of lives.

There is a lot more involved than just taking your nice friendly pooch to someone's bedside. Doing therapy dog work involves your own emotional stability as well as that of your dog. But once you have met all the requirements for this work, making the rounds once a week or once a month with your therapy dog is possibly the most rewarding of all community activities.

Disaster Aid

This community service is definitely not for everyone, partly because it is time-consuming. The initial training is rigorous, and there can be no let-up in the continuing workouts, because members are on call 24 hours a day to go wherever they are needed at a moment's notice. But if you think you would like to be able to assist in a disaster, look into search-and-rescue work. The network of search-and-rescue volunteers is worldwide, and all members of the American Rescue Dog Association (ARDA) who are qualified to do this work are volunteers who train and maintain their own dogs.

Physical Aid

Most people are familiar with Seeing Eye dogs, which serve as blind people's eyes, but not with all the other work that dogs are trained to do to assist the disabled. Dogs are also specially trained to pull wheelchairs, carry school books, pick up dropped objects, open and close doors. Some also are ears for the deaf. All these assistance-trained dogs, by the way, are allowed anywhere "No Pet" signs exist (as are therapy dogs when properly identified). Getting started in any of this fascinating work requires a background in dog training and canine behavior, but there are also volunteer jobs ranging from answering the phone to cleaning out kennels to providing a foster home for a puppy. You have only to ask.

Making the rounds with your therapy dog can be very rewarding.

part four

Beyond
the
Basics

chapter 12

Recommended Reading

Books

ABOUT HEALTH CARE

Ackerman, Lowell. *Guide to Skin and Haircoat Problems in Dogs*. Loveland, Colo.: Alpine Publications, 1994.

Alderton, David. *The Dog Care Manual*. Hauppauge, N.Y.: Barron's Educational Series, Inc., 1986.

American Kennel Club. *American Kennel Club Dog Care and Training*. New York: Howell Book House, 1991.

Bamberger, Michelle, DVM. *Help! The Quick Guide to First Aid for Your Dog*. New York: Howell Book House, 1995.

Carlson, Delbert, DVM, and James Giffin, MD. *Dog Owner's Home Veterinary Handbook*. New York: Howell Book House, 1992.

DeBitetto, James, DVM, and Sarah Hodgson. *You & Your Puppy*. New York: Howell Book House, 1995.

Humphries, Jim, DVM. *Dr. Jim's Animal Clinic for Dogs*. New York: Howell Book House, 1994.

McGinnis, Terri. *The Well Dog Book*. New York: Random House, 1991.

Pitcairn, Richard and Susan. *Natural Health for Dogs*. Emmaus, Pa.: Rodale Press, 1982.

ABOUT DOG SHOWS

Hall, Lynn. *Dog Showing for Beginners*. New York: Howell Book House, 1994.

Nichols, Virginia Tuck. *How to Show Your Own Dog*. Neptune, N. J.: TFH, 1970.

Vanacore, Connie. *Dog Showing, An Owner's Guide*. New York: Howell Book House, 1990.

ABOUT TRAINING

Ammen, Amy. *Training in No Time*. New York: Howell Book House, 1995.

Baer, Ted. *Communicating With Your Dog*. Hauppauge, N.Y.: Barron's Educational Series, Inc., 1989.

Benjamin, Carol Lea. *Dog Problems*. New York: Howell Book House, 1989.

Benjamin, Carol Lea. *Dog Training for Kids*. New York: Howell Book House, 1988.

Benjamin, Carol Lea. *Mother Knows Best*. New York: Howell Book House, 1985.

Benjamin, Carol Lea. *Surviving Your Dog's Adolescence*. New York: Howell Book House, 1993.

Bohnenkamp, Gwen. *Manners for the Modern Dog*. San Francisco: Perfect Paws, 1990.

Dibra, Bashkim. *Dog Training by Bash*. New York: Dell, 1992.

Dunbar, Ian, PhD, MRCVS. *Dr. Dunbar's Good Little Dog Book*, James & Kenneth Publishers, 2140 Shattuck Ave. #2406, Berkeley, Calif. 94704. (510) 658–8588. Order from the publisher.

Dunbar, Ian, PhD, MRCVS. *How to Teach a New Dog Old Tricks*, James & Kenneth Publishers. Order from the publisher; address above.

Dunbar, Ian, PhD, MRCVS, and Gwen Bohnenkamp. Booklets on *Preventing Aggression; Housetraining; Chewing; Digging; Barking; Socialization; Fearfulness; and Fighting*, James & Kenneth Publishers. Order from the publisher; address above.

Evans, Job Michael. *People, Pooches and Problems*. New York: Howell Book House, 1991.

Kilcommons, Brian and Sarah Wilson. *Good Owners, Great Dogs*. New York: Warner Books, 1992.

McMains, Joel M. *Dog Logic—Companion Obedience*. New York: Howell Book House, 1992.

Rutherford, Clarice and David H. Neil, MRCVS. *How to Raise a Puppy You Can Live With*. Loveland, Colo.: Alpine Publications, 1982.

Volhard, Jack and Melissa Bartlett. *What All Good Dogs Should Know: The Sensible Way to Train*. New York: Howell Book House, 1991.

ABOUT BREEDING

Harris, Beth J. Finder. *Breeding a Litter, The Complete Book of Prenatal and Postnatal Care*. New York: Howell Book House, 1983.

Holst, Phyllis, DVM. *Canine Reproduction*. Loveland, Colo.: Alpine Publications, 1985.

Walkowicz, Chris and Bonnie Wilcox, DVM. *Successful Dog Breeding, The Complete Handbook of Canine Midwifery*. New York: Howell Book House, 1994.

ABOUT ACTIVITIES

American Rescue Dog Association. *Search and Rescue Dogs*. New York: Howell Book House, 1991.

Barwig, Susan and Stewart Hilliard. *Schutzhund*. New York: Howell Book House, 1991.

Beaman, Arthur S. *Lure Coursing*. New York: Howell Book House, 1994.

Daniels, Julie. *Enjoying Dog Agility—From Backyard to Competition*. New York: Doral Publishing, 1990.

Davis, Kathy Diamond. *Therapy Dogs*. New York: Howell Book House, 1992.

Gallup, Davis Anne. *Running With Man's Best Friend*. Loveland, Colo.: Alpine Publications, 1986.

Habgood, Dawn and Robert. *On the Road Again With Man's Best Friend*. New England, Mid-Atlantic, West Coast and Southeast editions. Selective guides to area bed and breakfasts, inns, hotels and resorts that welcome guests and their dogs. New York: Howell Book House, 1995.

Holland, Vergil S. *Herding Dogs*. New York: Howell Book House, 1994.

LaBelle, Charlene G. *Backpacking With Your Dog*. Loveland, Colo.: Alpine Publications, 1993.

Simmons-Moake, Jane. *Agility Training, The Fun Sport for All Dogs*. New York: Howell Book House, 1991.

Spencer, James B. *Hup! Training Flushing Spaniels the American Way*. New York: Howell Book House, 1992.

Spencer, James B. *Point! Training the All-Seasons Birddog*. New York: Howell Book House, 1995.

Tarrant, Bill. *Training the Hunting Retriever*. New York: Howell Book House, 1991.

Volhard, Jack and Wendy. *The Canine Good Citizen*. New York: Howell Book House, 1994.

General Titles

Haggerty, Captain Arthur J. *How to Get Your Pet Into Show Business*. New York: Howell Book House, 1994.

McLennan, Bardi. *Dogs and Kids, Parenting Tips*. New York: Howell Book House, 1993.

Moran, Patti J. *Pet Sitting for Profit, A Complete Manual for Professional Success*. New York: Howell Book House, 1992.

Scalisi, Danny and Libby Moses. *When Rover Just Won't Do, Over 2,000 Suggestions for Naming Your Dog.* New York: Howell Book House, 1993.

Sife, Wallace, PhD. *The Loss of a Pet.* New York: Howell Book House, 1993.

Wrede, Barbara J. *Civilizing Your Puppy.* Hauppauge, N.Y.: Barron's Educational Series, 1992.

Magazines

The AKC GAZETTE, The Official Journal for the Sport of Purebred Dogs. American Kennel Club, 51 Madison Ave., New York, NY.

Bloodlines Journal. United Kennel Club, 100 E. Kilgore Rd., Kalamazoo, MI.

Dog Fancy. Fancy Publications, 3 Burroughs, Irvine, CA 92718

Dog World. Maclean Hunter Publishing Corp., 29 N. Wacker Dr., Chicago, IL 60606.

Videos

"SIRIUS Puppy Training," by Ian Dunbar, PhD, MRCVS. James & Kenneth Publishers, 2140 Shattuck Ave. #2406, Berkeley, CA 94704. Order from the publisher.

"Training the Companion Dog," from Dr. Dunbar's British TV Series, James & Kenneth Publishers. (See address above).

The American Kennel Club produces videos on every breed of dog, as well as on hunting tests, field trials and other areas of interest to purebred dog owners. For more information, write to AKC/Video Fulfillment, 5580 Centerview Dr., Suite 200, Raleigh, NC 27606.

chapter 13

Resources

Breed Clubs

Every breed recognized by the American Kennel Club has a national (parent) club. National clubs are a great source of information on your breed. You can get the name of the secretary of the club by contacting:

The American Kennel Club
51 Madison Avenue
New York, NY 10010
(212) 696-8200

There are also numerous all-breed, individual breed, obedience, hunting and other special-interest dog clubs across the country. The American Kennel Club can provide you with a geographical list of clubs to find ones in your area. Contact them at the above address.

Registry Organizations

Registry organizations register purebred dogs. The American Kennel Club is the oldest and largest in this country, and currently recognizes over 130 breeds. The United Kennel Club registers some breeds the AKC doesn't (including the American Pit Bull Terrier and the Miniature Fox Terrier) as well as many of the same breeds. The others included here are for your reference; the AKC can provide you with a list of foreign registries.

American Kennel Club
51 Madison Avenue
New York, NY 10010

United Kennel Club (UKC)
100 E. Kilgore Road
Kalamazoo, MI 49001-5598

American Dog Breeders Assn.
P.O. Box 1771
Salt Lake City, UT 84110
(Registers American Pit Bull Terriers)

Canadian Kennel Club
89 Skyway Avenue
Etobicoke, Ontario
Canada M9W 6R4

National Stock Dog Registry
P.O. Box 402
Butler, IN 46721
(Registers working stock dogs)

Orthopedic Foundation for Animals (OFA)
2300 E. Nifong Blvd.
Columbia, MO 65201-3856
(Hip registry)

Activity Clubs

Write to these organizations for information on the
activities they sponsor.

American Kennel Club
51 Madison Avenue
New York, NY 10010
(Conformation Shows, Obedience Trials, Field
Trials and Hunting Tests, Agility, Canine Good

Citizen, Lure Coursing, Herding, Tracking, Earthdog Tests, Coonhunting.)

United Kennel Club
100 E. Kilgore Road
Kalamazoo, MI 49001-5598
(Conformation Shows, Obedience Trials, Agility, Hunting for Various Breeds, Terrier Trials and more.)

North American Flyball Assn.
1342 Jeff St.
Ypsilanti, MI 48198

International Sled Dog Racing Assn.
P.O. Box 446
Norman, ID 83848-0446

North American Working Dog Assn., Inc.
Southeast Kreisgruppe
P.O. Box 833
Brunswick, GA 31521

Trainers

Association of Pet Dog Trainers
P.O. Box 3734
Salinas, CA 93912
(408) 663–9257

American Dog Trainers' Network
161 West 4th St.
New York, NY 10014
(212) 727–7257

National Association of Dog Obedience Instructors
2286 East Steel Rd.
St. Johns, MI 48879

Associations

American Dog Owners Assn.
1654 Columbia Tpk.
Castleton, NY 12033
(Combats anti-dog legislation)

Delta Society
P.O. Box 1080
Renton, WA 98057-1080
(Promotes the human/animal bond through
pet-assisted therapy and other programs)

Dog Writers Assn. of America (DWAA)
Sally Cooper, Secy.
222 Woodchuck Ln.
Harwinton, CT 06791

National Assn. for Search and Rescue (NASAR)
P.O. Box 3709
Fairfax, VA 22038

Therapy Dogs International
1536 Morris Place
Hillside, NJ 07205